The National Underwriter Company

PERSONAL UMBRELLA COVERAGE GUIDE, 2ND EDITION

By Diane W. Richardson, CPCU

Highlights of the *Personal Umbrella Coverage Guide, 2nd Edition*

This fully revised and updated second edition of our popular ***Personal Umbrella Coverage Guide*** continues—and builds on—all the features that made this book the instant, must-have resource for insurance professionals handling personal lines.

The book gives a complete overview of personal umbrella insurance. As umbrella forms vary from carrier to carrier, this practical resource reviews the ISO, AAIS and MSO forms highlighting both their similarities and differences. It makes clear when and why umbrella policies are necessary and valuable. It thoroughly analyzes underlying coverages as they relate to obtaining umbrella coverage and providing full protection to the insured. Potential gaps are highlighted, and endorsements that may cover these gaps are discussed. The difference between excess and umbrella coverage is explained. Plus, eligibility requirements, definitions, conditions and exclusions are reviewed.

In addition, this new, second edition now includes:

- Explanations of updated policy forms
- Chapter on exclusions
- Discussion of MSO forms
- Analysis of newly added exclusions, including those surrounding the internet, Facebook, Twitter, electronic aggression, and more—with expert analysis of relevant cases
- Examination of pollution and pollutants

And this book delivers a full analysis of who qualifies as insured, including non-spouse residents, foster children, children split between residences and trusts, and coverage for those in assisted living centers.

Plus—the ISO, AAIS and MSO umbrella forms are all in the book.

In short, the fully updated and completely current ***Personal Umbrella Coverage Guide, 2nd Edition***, enables you to guide every client through the *specifics* of obtaining the umbrella policy appropriate for them—and expand your personal-lines book of business in the process.

For customer service questions or to place additional orders, please call 1-800-543-0874.

Coverage Guides Also Available:

- Businessowners Policy
- Business Income
- Commercial Auto Program
- Commercial General Liability
- Commercial Property
- Condominium Insurance Coverage
- Construction Defects
- Critical Issues in CGL
- Directors and Officers Liability
- Employment Practices Liability
- Guide to Captives and Alternative Risk Financing
- Homeowners
- Insurance Claims
- Mold Claims
- Personal Auto Policy
- Workers Compensation

2nd Edition

Personal Umbrella Coverage Guide

Personal Lines Series

Diane W. Richardson, CPCU

The National Underwriter Company

International Standard Book Number: 978-1-941627-71-6

Library of Congress Control Number: 2016939967

Printed in the United States of America

About The National Underwriter Company

For over 110 years, The National Underwriter Company has been the first in line with the targeted tax, insurance, and financial planning information you need to make critical business decisions. Boasting nearly a century of expert experience, our reputable Editors are dedicated to putting accurate and relevant information right at your fingertips. With *Tax Facts*, *Tools & Techniques*, *National Underwriter Advanced Markets*, *Field Guide*, *FC&S*®, *FC&S Legal* and other resources available in print, eBook, CD, and online, you can be assured that as the industry evolves National Underwriter will be at the forefront with the thorough and easy-to-use resources you rely on for success.

The National Underwriter Company Update Service Notification

This National Underwriter Company publication is regularly updated to include coverage of developments and changes that affect the content. If you did not purchase this publication directly from The National Underwriter Company and you want to receive these important updates sent on a 30-day review basis and billed separately, please contact us at (800) 543-0874. Or you can mail your request with your name, company, address, and the title of the book to:

The National Underwriter Company
4157 Olympic Boulevard
Suite 225
Erlanger, KY 41018

If you purchased this publication from The National Underwriter Company directly, you have already been registered for the update service.

National Underwriter Company Contact Information

To order any National Underwriter Company title, please

- call 1-800-543-0874, 8-6 ET Monday – Thursday and 8 to 5 ET Friday
- online bookstore at www.nationalunderwriter.com, or
- mail to The National Underwriter Company, Orders Department, 4157 Olympic Blvd., Ste. 225, Erlanger, KY 41018

About the Authors

Diane W. Richardson, CPCU, began her insurance career as a personal lines underwriter. She also worked as a state filings supervisor and as an agent. Diane retired from The National Underwriter Company, where she was an Associate Editor of *FC&S Bulletins*. She continues to consult for *FC&S*.

Her publications include *Insuring to Value* (co-authored with Marshall-Swift/Boeck), *The Homeowners Coverage Guide* (First through Fifth Editions), *The Personal Umbrella Coverage Guide*, and *The Home-Based Business Coverage Guide*.

She earned a BA from the University of Vermont and an EdM from Harvard.

Publisher

Kelly B. Maheu, J.D., is Vice President in charge of the Practical Insights Division of ALM Media, which produces The National Underwriter's professional publications. Kelly has been with The National Underwriter Company since 2006, and has served as the Managing Director of The National Underwriter's Professional Publishing Division as well as performing editorial, content acquisition, and product development roles.

Prior to joining The National Underwriter Company, Kelly worked in the legal and insurance fields for LexisNexis®, Progressive Insurance, and a Cincinnati insurance defense litigation firm.

Kelly has edited and contributed to numerous books and publications including the *Personal Auto Insurance Policy Coverage Guide*, *Cyberliability and Insurance*, *The National Underwriter Sales Essentials Series*, and *The Tools and Techniques of Risk Management for Financial Planners*.

Kelly earned her law degree from The University of Cincinnati College of Law and holds a BA from Miami University, Ohio, with a double major in English/Journalism and Psychology.

Managing Editor

Christine G. Barlow, CPCU, is Managing Editor of Online *FC&S Bulletins* of The National Underwriter Company, an ALM Media company. Christine has been with The National Underwriter Company since 2006, when she began as an assistant editor. Before joining the National

Underwriter Company, she was an underwriting supervisor for Maryland Automobile Insurance Fund, underwriter for Montgomery Mutual Insurance Company, senior underwriter for Old American, and an underwriter for Charter Group.

The publications Christine wrote or edited include *Personal Lines Unlocked*, *The Key to Personal Lines Underwriting*, *Homeowners Personal Lines Coverage Guide*, *Closing the Gap*, and *Condominium Insurance Coverage Guide*, all published by The National Underwriter Company. Christine also writes articles for Claims magazine. She is a speaker or presenter at various insurance related seminars and meetings.

Christine graduated cum laude from Towson University, Maryland, with a degree in Sociology/Psychology and a concentration in Gerontology.

Editorial Services

Connie L. Jump, Manager, Editorial Operations.

Emily Brunner, Editorial Assistant.

Preface

The Personal Umbrella Book

As of this writing (November, 2015*), the stock market is reaching new heights. Silicon Valley produces millionaires almost exponentially. Persons who began work a little over ten years ago at some rapid-growth companies can retire in their mid-forties; a heretofore unheard-of phenomena. New wealth is being created, and, along with that wealth comes the need to protect it. When the preface to the Personal Umbrella Book was first written in November 2000, the market was at 10,602.95. November 12th's close: 17,448.07. So, the emphasis on an umbrella as one method of wealth protection is just as true today as it was fifteen years ago.

Obviously an umbrella insurance policy is not the only wealth protection vehicle available. There are many financial products on the market. But these products will not protect the new millionaire in event of a lawsuit alleging bodily or personal injury or property damage. Unfortunately, wealthy individuals are often targets. Who would be more likely to be sued in event of a car accident, Bill Gates (yes, *that* Bill Gates) or Suzy Gates, proud driver of a 2005 Honda?

This is not to say that only the wealthy are targets. Far from it. In today's litigious society, anyone is fair game. In 2012, the most recent year for which statistics are available, there were over 96 million civil suits filed in the state courts (National Center for State Courts). This is up from the 15,400,000 noted in the first edition. For the same period, there were 280,281 pending in the federal courts, which is only slightly higher than the 272,027 number noted in the first edition (Statistical Division of U.S. Courts). An umbrella can serve to protect the assets for the wealthy, and those who simply do not wish to see their assets drained because of a lawsuit.

As the need for a personal umbrella becomes greater, so does the need for the insurance professional to understand the concept and the forms. Although the Insurance Services Office (ISO) introduced a personal umbrella form in 1998, most insurers had by then already filed their own forms, and continue to use them, although insurers often incorporate some of the ISO wording into their own umbrella forms. The reason for this is that the courts have already adjudicated much of the ISO language, and so it is to an insurer's advantage to not have to reinvent the wheel, so to speak. In this book we will be reviewing the ISO personal liability policy DL 98 01 02 15 (the first edition reviewed DL 98 01 06 98).

The American Association of Insurance Services (AAIS) released a personal umbrella form in 2000, and revised the form in 2011. It is this form, PU 0001 10 11, that we will be reviewing in this edition.

Finally, the Mutual Services Office (MSO) offers a personal umbrella MPL 100 01 12. We will be including this form as well.

Knowing what coverages are provided – indeed, even knowing where to look for the coverages (and the exclusions of coverage) in any one given form – is vital. It's too late after a claim has been presented to learn that there is no coverage, even though the term "umbrella" has led the insured to believe that coverage exists.

The purpose of this book is to acquaint the insurance professional with the common provisions, conditions, and coverages found in several personal umbrella forms. Where there are distinctive exclusions or differences in wording that lead to coverage variations, these are addressed as well. Only through understanding what is, and is not, covered, can the professional do the best job possible for the client.

One final note: remember that umbrella forms are intended to form a part of an insured's total insurance package. For this reason, and because the umbrella is intended to build upon other coverages, it is important to have a grasp of those *other coverages*—be they auto, homeowners, boatowners, motorcycles, etc. If you are unsure about the basic underlying coverages, review the underlying policy(ies). Assumptions can be disastrous.

*Editorial note: January 2016 has seen the market go down nearly 2,000 points; however, overall, the market has been up.

Table of Contents

Chapter 1

An Umbrella Overview

Why an Umbrella?

Auto and homeowners policies provide adequate liability protection for many people. Why, therefore, would anyone purchase an umbrella liability policy? The primary reason is to protect personal assets. Umbrellas provide an extra layer of liability coverage beyond that offered by homeowners, renters, personal auto, or stand alone personal liability policies.

Think of a young couple starting out. Both work and their combined income is good. However, being prudent, they drive older cars and save their money to purchase a home. A child enters the picture; then another. Both parents continue to work.

Because the family's income level rises, they are able to afford new vehicles and enjoy an increasingly affluent lifestyle. Since the family lives close to a large body of water, it seems reasonable to purchase a 22 foot, 150 HP inboard-out drive. (Note: see ISO homeowners liability exclusion B.2.c; AAIS exclusion 8.a.3; and MSO incidental watercraft liability coverage.) The whole family enjoys a day on the water. A condo at their favorite winter vacation spot is the next purchase. It will pay for itself since they intend to rent it out during the time they don't use it themselves. (Is separate coverage in order? If yes, do they have it?)

The condo is near a large winter resort area, so naturally two snowmobiles (his 'n hers) are the next purchases. They decide to allow anyone renting the condo to have access to the snowmobiles. (Refer to ISO exclusion A.2.d; AAIS 7.a.4; and MSO incidental land vehicle coverage 7.B.)

In the meantime, the children are growing up. The oldest, a boy, has gotten his drivers' license, and his parents have purchased a car, a four-door sedan, for him to drive to school and to his after-school job. After two years, the next child, a girl, begins to drive and her parents purchase a car for her as well.

However, she is not the safe, careful driver her brother is. She likes nothing better than to pile several of her friends in the car and cruise around. A favorite activity is to text her friends in the back seat while driving—after all, she has one hand on the wheel! She loses control of the car, and it plows into an oncoming car. A passenger in the other vehicle is killed, and two of the daughter's friends are critically injured. One recovers, but one will be paralyzed for life from the waist down.

The family's auto policy has limits for bodily injury of $100,000 per person and $300,000 per accident; and $100,000 property damage limits. The policy pays its limits, and then bows out of the picture. Homeowners liability does not apply in circumstances such as these. But the fact that the auto policy has maxed out its limits does not stop a lawsuit from the estate of the passenger in the oncoming vehicle and friendship does not prevent a suit from the paralyzed friend's parents. After all, the family has assets (home, condo, boat, vehicles, etc.) that can be attached.

A bleak picture? Never happen?

If it seems melodramatic, consider the picture *without* the daughter's accident. What about the condo with the snowmobiles? What happens if someone runs the snowmobile into a tree, seriously injuring himself, and sues the owner for negligence? The condo owner should have known the renter didn't know how to drive a snowmobile! Or perhaps one day the son takes a few of his buddies out on the boat. As they playfully wrestle to see who can take over the wheel, the boat goes out of control and plows into a marina, totaling a Donzi 38 (2016 list price $350,000) and seriously damaging a pontoon boat, which just happens to have a family on-board. The family's boat owners policy has $100/300 BI and $100,000 property damage limits.

Having a personal umbrella in place might have helped alleviate some of the financial loss, as well as contribute toward defense costs.

If an imaginary scenario does not convince you of the need for an umbrella, consider this. Although the number of deaths of thirteen through nineteen-year-olds in auto accidents has decreased since 1975, the number of fatalities of drivers and passengers age thirteen through nineteen accounts for 56 percent of all drivers and passengers. Males age twenty through twenty-four accounted for 13.6 per 100,000; females 5.1. We cannot, however, view statistics for young drivers without taking a look at statistics for older drivers. Drivers over age seventy account for 1 percent of fatalities; this number sharply increases from age eighty-five up. Although the elderly drive fewer miles, age makes any injury—broken bones, for example—more severe[1]. This is not to say, necessarily, that older drivers *cause* more accidents—they don't—but if they are driving with friends in their age group any accident will result in more severe injuries.

With the youthful operator, it is the parents' assets that must be protected; with the elderly driver, it is their own.

Sometimes an umbrella policy can involve itself in unforeseen ways. As of this writing, several states require that uninsured/underinsured motorist coverage be offered on an umbrella policy. Among them are: Arizona, Kansas, Louisiana, Nevada, Alaska, West Virginia, Wisconsin, North Carolina, and Ohio. New Hampshire revised statutes 259:61 and 264:15 indicate the coverage must be offered, but in the case of *United Services Auto Association v. Wilkinson,* 569 A.2d 749 (New Hampshire 1989), the court held, with one dissention, that that had not been the intent of the legislature.

Note, though, that because a state does not require the coverage to be offered, it is not an indication that purchasing it is not a good idea. For just a few extra dollars, the policyholder can purchase an extra million (or whatever limits are selected according to the insurer's manual) of uninsured/underinsured motorist coverage.

In the case of *Nationwide Mutual Insurance Co. v. Chivington et al.,* 595 N.E.2d 1002 (Ohio 1991), the appellate court held that the insured's personal umbrella policy's uninsured/underinsured motorist coverage must contribute when the insured's parents were killed in an auto accident. Brenton Chivington, who lived with his parents, had both his own auto policy and a personal umbrella policy. When his parents were killed, the negligent driver's policy paid $200,000. The parents' policy, which had limits of $300,000 in uninsured/underinsured coverage, paid $100,000. The son therefore turned to his own auto policy, which provided $500,000 in uninsured/underinsured motorist coverage, and to his umbrella, which provided $1 million in uninsured/underinsured coverage. Since he had already received $300,000, his auto policy tendered $200,000; the umbrella the remaining $500,000 for a total of $1 million. (Note that uninsured/underinsured motorist coverage accrues not only for the benefit of an insured who is physically injured in an accident, but also for the benefit of someone entitled to receive damages from the person causing the bodily injury to the insured. The insured thus has a derivative claim. See the personal auto policy [PAP] Part C.B.3., which says that "insured" means "any person for damages that person is entitled to recover because of 'bodily injury' to which this coverage applies sustained by a person described in 1. or 2. above." The person described in 1. or 2. means "you or any 'family member'," or "any other person 'occupying' 'your covered auto'.")

In the states that require that uninsured/underinsured motorist coverage be offered on an umbrella, this case makes a strong selling point for the parents of young children to purchase an umbrella.

What Is an Umbrella?

An umbrella policy provides worldwide liability coverage over and above that provided by underlying policies. For most personal lines clients, these underlying policies will be auto and homeowners. The liability coverage may be excess, or it may be "drop down". Think of a collapsed folding umbrella. When the umbrella begins to open, the shaft lengthens. That is the excess portion; the part of the umbrella that provides liability coverage over that which is already in place.

But an umbrella can provide more coverage than an excess form. As the umbrella opens, the cloth stretches over the spokes in a kind of inverted scallop pattern, protecting a much greater area than that protected by just the umbrella shaft. This broader area of coverage, that protects even where there is no underlying coverage, is often referred to as "drop down," because it drops down to protect where no underlying coverage exists. It is this "drop down" feature that distinguishes a true umbrella from an excess policy.

For example, if an insured's auto policy has limits of $250,000/$500,000 bodily injury and $250,000 property damage, when added to a $1 million umbrella the insured now has limits of $1,250,000/$1,500,000/$1,250,000. If the insured has $100,000 personal liability coverage on his or her homeowners, then, with the umbrella, there is a total of $1,100,000 in coverage. For covered occurrences not afforded coverage by the underlying policies (homeowners policies commonly do not provide personal injury coverage unless it is added by endorsement; umbrella policies include this coverage as a matter of course) the umbrella provides $1 million or whatever limit is selected, subject to the retained limit (discussed below).

What Do Umbrellas Have In Common?

Lack of State Regulation

As of this writing, few states specifically regulate (with the exception of requiring that uninsured/underinsured motorist coverage be offered) personal umbrellas. Two states are Texas and New York. Texas requires ten days' notice of cancellation for nonpayment of premium, change in operations resulting in a hazard, or when continuation would place the insurer in violation of the Texas insurance code; otherwise forty-five days' notice is required. New York regulates "personal lines insurance," such as homeowners and umbrellas, as well as auto insurance. An insurer may cancel upon giving at least forty-five days' notice. Cancellation reasons include nonpayment of premium, conviction of a crime increasing the hazard insured against, discovery or fraud or material misrepresentation, or willful or reckless acts or omissions increasing the hazard insured against.

However, the state mandates a “required policy period” of three years from the date the policy is first issued or voluntarily renewed. Nonrenewal may be only for the cancellation reasons, unless the insurer no longer does business in the state.

In nonregulated states, an insurer may cancel for any reason, although, of course, the reason must be a legitimate one, such as an increase in hazard. Depending upon the insurer, generally ten days is given for nonpayment of premium; thirty days for any other reason. Notice of nonrenewal is generally thirty days.

Other states regulate personal insurance, though, which may include umbrellas. For example, in Oklahoma a liability policy cannot be retroactively annulled based on agreement between insured and insurer. In both Oregon and Washington, credit scores may not be used as sole reasons to decline to issue policies.

Umbrellas are perceived as nonessential insurance, unlike auto insurance, which is tied to state-mandated financial responsibility laws, or homeowners insurance, which is tied to lending institutions’ requirements. Perhaps because of this, state regulators have been hesitant to become involved. Also, until recently each insurer developed its own form. In 1998 Insurance Services Office (ISO) developed a personal umbrella policy, followed in 2000 by the American Association of Insurance Services (AAIS); however, many insurers continue to use their own forms. Therefore, the coverages and exclusions found in personal umbrellas vary from insurer to insurer.

There are, however, some common elements in umbrellas. All contain definitions, an insuring agreement, coverages (and exclusions), miscellaneous conditions, the duty to defend, and the requirement to maintain underlying insurance. The first four common elements will be discussed in later chapters.

Duty to Defend

Often the cost of defending against a suit or claim can represent a significant expense. Umbrella policies provide defense coverage that is in addition to the limit of liability. The umbrella insurer frequently has the right to join in a defense with an underlying insurance carrier if it appears the umbrella coverage will be triggered, and sometimes will take over a defense if the underlying policy limits have been exhausted.

When a claim is outside the scope of the insurance policy’s coverage, the insurer has no duty to defend. However, the duty to defend is broader than the duty to indemnify. So, if *any* allegations can be brought within the scope of the coverage, then the insurer owes the duty. As an appellate court stated, applying Missouri law, "An insurer's duty to defend exists when the petition in the underlying action states some grounds of liability covered by its insurance policy. Therefore, we must compare 'the language of the insurance contract and the allegations of the petition in the action brought by the person injured or damaged. If the complaint alleges facts which state a claim *potentially* (italics added) within the policy's coverage, there is a duty to defend.'"

In the case of *Lowell K. Wood v. Safeco Insurance Company of America,* 980 S.W.2d 43 (Missouri 1998), the insured owned real estate along a river in Missouri. He sold the property to another; following the sale, the property flooded twice. The insured was sued for alleged intentional misrepresentations and negligent misrepresentation. The buyer dismissed that suit, but then filed another lawsuit alleging fraud due to intentional misrepresentations and negligent misrepresentations. This suit was dismissed with prejudice. The insured's umbrella insurer refused to defend either suit; the insured filed a damages action against his insurer.

At trial, the insurer argued that it was not required to defend for two reasons. First, the claims were not "occurrences" as defined by the policy ("'Occurrence' means an accident, including continuous or repeated exposure to substantially the same general harmful conditions, which results, during the coverage period, in 'personal injury' or 'property damage…'"). Second, the claims were excluded because of the "expected or intended" acts exclusion.

The trial court found for the insurer. But on appeal, the court ruled for the insured, holding that the negligent misrepresentations were indeed an "occurrence" by definition, which resulted in the buyer's loss of use of the property, which was within the definition of property damage. Therefore, the insurer owed a duty to defend. This case will be discussed again in connection with the definition of "occurrence" in the next chapter, because in it the court considered several other jurisdictions' views.

Underlying Insurance Requirements

Umbrellas are designed to provide coverage over and above that provided by underlying policies, except, of course, when they respond to covered occurrences not addressed by the underlying insurance. The requirement to maintain underlying insurance is found within the conditions of any given umbrella form. Some insurers include as well the specific amounts of underlying insurance they require. These amounts vary. For example, one insurer may require auto liability limits of $100,000/$300,000 bodily injury and $100,000 property damage; another

$100,000/$300,000/$50,000. Most insurers require at least $100,000 underlying comprehensive personal liability, although some will accept $50,000 while yet another insurer insists on $300,000. Requirements for underlying coverage for watercraft, recreational motor vehicles (other than motorcycles) and aircraft (if the underwriting guidelines allow an umbrella to be written over this exposure) vary from insurer to insurer as well.

Retained Limit

The term "retained limit" refers not only to what may be thought of as a deductible, but to the underlying limits of insurance as well. For example, a common retained limit on an umbrella is $250. So, in the event of a covered auto liability loss, the insured "retains," through the underlying policy, whatever amount is required, plus the $250. Say, for example, the insured is required to maintain $300,000 single limit auto liability, and the umbrella has a $250 retained limit. A covered claim is made for $500,000. The insured "retains" $300,250 of the loss, although $300,000 of it will be covered by the underlying auto insurance. Some insurers have two retained limits, one where the claim *is* covered by underlying insurance, and another where the umbrella will provide primary coverage.

What happens if the insured fails to maintain the required underlying limit of insurance? Does the umbrella then respond on a primary basis? Generally, no. The umbrella forms usually contain language stating that the policy will still respond to a covered claim, but only to the extent it would have had the insured maintain the necessary underlying limits. This was made clear in the case of *Centennial Insurance Company v. Robert Krutek and Richard Naylor,* 1992 U.S. Dist. Lexis 19220 (Illinois 1992). In this case, Robert Krutek allegedly negligently injured Richard Naylor in an auto accident. Robert Krutek's father, with whom he resided, had an umbrella policy with limits of $2,000,000. Robert qualified as an insured under the umbrella; however, he had his own auto insurance with a bodily injury liability limit of $20,000. The umbrella required underlying auto coverage of at least $300,000 combined single limits.

The court found that the policy language was clear. The insuring agreement stated that the policy applied only in excess of the retained limit. The retained limit was defined as "the total of the applicable limits of the underlying policy(ies) listed or insurance described in Schedule A… and the applicable limits of any other underlying insurance collectible by the insured." "Retained limit" was further defined as the greater of either the above amount or $250. The court made this additional point: that the wording "applicable limit" refers to the type, rather than the collectability, of the policy. Therefore, ruled the court, the Centennial umbrella would not apply until the amount of $320,000 in damages was reached.

A similar case is that of *State Farm Fire and Casualty Co. v. Nationwide Mutual Insurance Co.,* 596 F. Supp. 2d 940 (E.D. VI 2009). Robert Hoag hit and injured a pedestrian. He owned a vehicle insured with State Farm with bodily injury limits of $25,000. However, he resided with his father, and so was covered under his father's umbrella (also with State Farm). The pedestrian made claim through her own auto insurer, Nationwide, for underinsured coverage. Nationwide said that the gap in underinsured coverage should be covered through Hoag's father's umbrella. The State Farm umbrella policy explicitly stated, "We may not provide coverage if you refuse to…maintain your underlying insurance." (Note, "may" in a contract of insurance always means "have permission to," and not "we might" [or might not].) Therefore, ruled the court, the pedestrian's claim was denied.

However, in the case of *Israel v. State Farm*, 789 A.2d 974 (CT 2002), even though Israel had no underlying UM/UIM coverage, still the court found he could collect on his mother's and stepfather's umbrella when his wife was killed in an auto accident in Florida. This case is also notable because Israel lived with his mother and stepfather part of the year in Connecticut, and the remainder of the year with his wife in Florida! This is explained by the fact that he was an airline pilot, and flew out of Connecticut. The court found that, under Connecticut state law, a person might have two residences.

As an aside, one of the most troubling things to undertake in the case of stepchildren is where, actually, they reside—with mother or with father? This dilemma occurs often when the child is involved in an auto accident. Courts normally look at where the child keeps belongings, attends school, receives mail, etc. All these components were present in the case of *Israel* with regard to both the Connecticut residence with his parents and the Florida residence with his wife and the court said that in Connecticut a person might have two residences. Note, though, that this is Connecticut law, and what is true there might not be true in, say, Indiana.

Effective Dates

The importance of watching policy dates was forcibly brought home in the case of *Commercial Union Insurance Co. v. Kevin M. Connors et al.,* 679 N.E.2d 1012 (1995). In this case, the insureds had an umbrella policy with an expiration date of November 30, 1989. Their son was involved in an at-fault accident on December 1, 1989, and died as a result. The injured party sued his estate. Although the son's auto policy responded, the umbrella insurer informed the insureds that the policy had expired. The insureds had placed coverage through a new agency; the new agent did not send an application for a new umbrella until November 28. Remember, many insurers will not allow an agent to bind umbrella coverage. Clearly, said the court, there was no coverage.

AAIS, for example, allows an umbrella to be written for a period of less than one year so as to achieve a common anniversary date with underlying policies, so if faced with different effective dates there are ways to achieve common dates.

Before submitting an umbrella application, check carefully with the insurer regarding underwriting criteria, underlying limits requirements, etc. Because of the amount of coverage involved (the least being $1 million), often umbrella applications must be submitted unbound. It is a good practice to make sure that all policies in question – homeowners, auto, watercraft, and umbrella – have concurrent dates. It is often easiest to make the inception date for an umbrella the same as the auto; the homeowners policy period can then be adjusted to coincide with the two others. If possible, it is even more desirable to have the same insurer for all coverages. That way, there is no question as to which policy should respond first in event of a loss, and the coverages and exclusions should be such that there are no gaps in coverage.

Eligibility Requirements

Before continuing to our discussion of the definitions in standard umbrella forms, we will give an overview of the eligibility requirements. Remember, though, that each insurer will no doubt have its own set of requirements. It is no small thing to promise a pay-out of a million dollars or more, so insurers carefully scrutinize applications.

First, we look at ISO. According to the umbrella manual, a personal umbrella policy may be issued to an individual, or spouses who are residents in the same household. Remember that in ISO homeowners endorsement HO 04 58 other members of your household will give liability coverage to a person scheduled on the declarations. However, this person would have to purchase his or her own umbrella. A personal umbrella policy may *not* be issued to cover any locations to which farm forms or rates apply under the rules of the company. An "adequate program" of underlying insurance, as determined by the insurer, must be maintained by the insured and scheduled on the declarations. Underlying coverage shall consist of: a homeowners or personal liability policy, or equivalent, and a personal auto policy, or equivalent. (Endorsement DL 98 11 may be used to waive auto policy requirements.) The personal umbrella policy must be written separately from any other policy form, including a homeowners, dwelling policy, personal liability policy, or personal auto policy.

AAIS, because it does not have an auto form, states "refer to company" with regard to the underlying auto policy. The homeowners form must be written on an AAIS form "or comparable" homeowners form. Because AAIS writes family farms, it allows farms to be written on a personal umbrella. However, it would bc wise to check with the insurer. The umbrella may be written on an aggregate basis if the underlying policy has aggregate limits. The underlying minimum limits required are: auto, 500,000 CSL or 250/500/100; personal liability, 300,000 per occurrence; unlicensed recreational vehicle, 300,000 per occurrence; watercraft, 300,000 per occurrence. The retained limit is $1,000.

MSO has a quite extensive list of ineligible exposures, among them: any underlying policy containing restrictive endorsements, such as an animal liability exclusion, that would cause the umbrella to become primary; auto driver with two or more moving violations or at-fault accidents in a three-year period; law enforcement officials; labor leaders; politicians, etc. Trampoline owners are also not eligible, as are those homeowners with unfenced pools or pools with diving boards or slides. For more information, consult the manual. Underlying required limits are: auto, 300/300/100 or 250/500/100 or 300 CSL, unless there is a youthful driver (under age twenty-five) with one moving violation within a three-year period, and then 500/500/100 or 500 CSL limits are required. UM/UIM must be the same as the auto limits, but this is available only in states where required by law or regulation. Personal liability must be 300,000; nonlicensed recreational vehicles, 300,000; watercraft liability, 300,000 (however watercraft greater than fifty feet or requiring a crew are not allowed); employers liability (where required by law or regulation), 100,000 per accident/100,000 each employee for BI by disease and 500,000 per policy for disease. The retained limit (deductible) is $250.

A Final Note

The following forms and editions are the ones referred to in this book: Insurance Services Office (ISO) homeowners May 2011, umbrella February 2015, and Personal Auto Policy (PAP) January 2005; American Association of Insurance Services homeowners 2008 and umbrella October 2011; Mutual Service Office homeowners January 2011 (note, though, that MSO uses a modular approach in assembling a policy, so the form to turn a homeowners into an HO-3 is dated January 01 05; the main property coverages form is dated January 2011), and the umbrella is January 2012.

Endnote

1. Insurance Institute for Highway Safety, iihs.org

Chapter 2

Definitions

Introduction

All umbrella forms contain definitions, the policy meaning of specified words or terms. Ideally, they should be identical to the definitions in the underlying policy(ies). But frequently they are not. And, indeed, whether or not a particular occurrence or event is covered is often first determined by checking the definitions. For example, a claimant alleges breach of fiduciary duty. A review of the definitions of "bodily injury," "personal injury," or "property damage," to which the umbrella coverage applies, indicates immediately that the umbrella is probably not the place to seek coverage.

In this chapter, we will look at how different forms define words or terms. Three different forms create the springboard for this discussion; these are representative of the other umbrella forms available. The Insurance Services Office (ISO) umbrella DL 98 01 02 15, the American Association of Insurance Services (AAIS) umbrella UM 0001 10 11, and the MSO umbrella MPL 100 01 12 forms are reprinted at the end of the book. The following definitions are common to all personal umbrella forms. Of course, there are others; these will be discussed later as we look at the various coverages and exclusions.

Bodily Injury

The first definition examined is "bodily injury." This is one of the most important definitions, because the umbrella, recall, promises to pay damages the insured is legally obligated to pay because of bodily injury or property damage arising out of a covered occurrence.

The ISO umbrella definition is:

"Bodily injury" means bodily harm, sickness or disease, including required care, loss of services and death that results.

The AAIS definition for "bodily injury" is:

"Bodily injury" means bodily harm to a person and includes sickness, disease, or death. This also includes required care and loss of services.

However, "bodily injury" does not mean bodily harm, sickness, disease, or death that arises out of mental or emotional injury, suffering, or distress that does not result from actual physical injury to a person.

In the second definition, we see "mental anguish" implied. One of the most vexatious questions frequently referred to a court of law for a determination is whether or not "bodily injury" encompasses mental injury – anguish, emotional distress, outrage, and the like. Some courts have attempted to reconcile the different points of view by holding that, when mental or emotional distress results in physical manifestation of bodily injury, a claim for damages falls within the scope of coverage. For example, in the case of *Trinity Universal Insurance Company et al. v. Nicole Cowan et al.*, 945 S.W.2d 819 (Texas 1997), the court examined whether a claim for mental anguish constituted "bodily injury" and thus triggered the insurer's duty to defend. In the policy in question, "bodily injury" was defined as "bodily harm, sickness or disease. This includes required care, loss of services and death that results." The Texas Supreme Court concluded that, "absent an allegation of physical manifestation of mental anguish, a claim of mental anguish is not a 'bodily injury' as defined in the policy for purposes of invoking the duty to defend."

The court in *Trinity* noted that a substantial majority of those courts considering the question have held that purely mental injuries do not constitute "bodily injury," and then added an impressive body of citations to verify this. The court also added citations documenting courts that held that purely emotional injury did, in fact, constitute "bodily injury." The point is, simply, that when considering whether there is coverage for emotional distress under the definition of "bodily injury" the jurisdiction must be considered.

Current judicial thinking, however, points to the direction that infliction of emotional distress, particularly when that infliction is intentional, will not be afforded coverage under the umbrella policy language. For example, in *Amica Mutual Insurance Company v. Vernon*, 2015 WL 1757642 (not reported in F.Supp.3d), the U.S. District Court for Idaho held that a worker's scathingly vicious card to a co-worker was not, as he claimed, just "social interaction." The co-worker committed suicide five days after received the card, but this was not, in the court's mind, "bodily injury" that conceivably could be covered by the umbrella. In the case of *Heacker v. Safeco Insurance Company of America, et al.*, 676 F.3d 724 (U.S. 8th 2012), the court found that the PTSD and alcoholism that Heacker claimed arose from the defendant's actions were not covered by either the defendant's homeowner's or her umbrella policy. The court said that the words "bodily injury" implied physical injury, and PTSD and alcoholism were not bodily sicknesses or diseases and therefore excluded from coverage. We will look at this case again when we discuss an "occurrence."

The MSO definition of "bodily injury" differs from the ISO and AAIS in that:

> *Bodily injury* means bodily harm, sickness, or disease sustained by a person during the coverage period, including death at any time, resulting from such, caused by a covered *occurrence*.

We will discuss this definition in more detail later in this chapter when we look at what constitutes an *occurrence*.

Property Damage

The personal umbrella coverage is triggered by bodily injury, personal injury, or *property damage* caused by a covered occurrence. The ISO umbrella definition is:

> "Property damage" means physical injury to, destruction of, or loss of use of tangible property.

This definition is a common one; indeed, the AAIS definition is similar. Also, it is like the definition for "property damage" contained in the ISO personal auto policy. The MSO definition differs:

> *Property damage* means the following which occurs during the policy period:
>
> 1. Direct injury to tangible property, including loss of use of such property (the loss of use is deemed to occur at the time of such direct physical injury).
>
> 2. Loss of use of tangible property that is not physically injured: all such loss of use is deemed to occur at the time of the *occurrence* causing the loss.

It is interesting that MSO identifies the time at which loss of use might occur. For example, an insured might negligently run into someone's home, but it is not discovered for over a day that the damage to the home precludes anyone being able to continue to reside there. With this definition, loss of use begins at the same moment the direct physical damage to the dwelling occurs.

In all definitions, coverage attaches when tangible property is physically injured or destroyed. Coverage also applies if the damaged property is no longer able to be used. So, for example, if an insured negligently crashes into an auto transport carrying six new Hyundai Sonatas (2016 MSRP starting at $21,750) so that all the vehicles except the carrier are totaled, the umbrella will respond to the property damage. If an insured negligently crashes into a row of rental cars, resulting in their being unable to be rented to customers, the umbrella responds to this loss of use. Should an insured negligently drive into the plate glass window of a large store so that the store is unable to open for a day while temporary repairs are being made, the policy responds to this loss of use.

In both these examples tangible property must be physically damaged for there to be coverage. What happens if the property suffers no damage, yet the owner is unable to use it because of an insured's action?

As all the definitions make clear, loss of use of tangible property that has not been physically injured is covered, so long as the loss of use arises from the covered actions of an insured—in other words, the actions causing the loss of use should not be intentional; that is to say, an insured cannot intend that the loss of use will occur. For example, the insured, while attempting to install a lawn sprinkler system, negligently cuts an underground phone line. Worse, he also cuts into a gas pipeline. The surrounding neighborhood, including a marina, must be evacuated while the gas leak is brought under control and the pressure checked. There is no damage to the neighboring property or the marina; but there is loss of use of the tangible property. Since the insured's negligence in this case is a covered occurrence (the definition of "occurrence" is discussed below), the resulting loss of use is covered up to the applicable limits.

Personal Injury

The next definition to be considered is that for "personal injury." "Personal injury" in insurance has traditionally referred to nonbodily injury; that is, injury to the mental well-being of the person. Use of the term to describe "bodily injury" has become more and more common, however. One need only look at the attorneys' ads in the yellow pages. ("Personal Injury! Workers' Compensation!" is the top line, followed by: "Auto/ Motorcycle Accidents, Dog Bites/Slip and Fall, Wrongful Death, Work Related Injuries…")

Check carefully to see that the umbrella clearly defines what the insurer means by "personal injury." Since many homeowners forms do not automatically include this coverage, it is one of the more important "drop down" coverages, and a powerful reason to purchase an umbrella. The coverage for personal injury is triggered by an offense (as defined below) committed during the policy period.

The ISO form defines "personal injury" thus:

"Personal injury" means injury arising out of one or more of the following offenses:

a. false arrest, detention or imprisonment;

b. malicious prosecution;

c. wrongful entry into, wrongful eviction from, or invasion of the right of private occupancy of a room, dwelling, or premises that a person occupies, if such offense is committed by or on behalf of the owner, landlord, or lessor of the room, dwelling, or premises; or

d. oral or written publication, including electronic publication, of material that:

   1) slanders or libels a person or an organization;

   2) disparages a person's or an organization's goods, products, or services; or

   3) violates a person's right of privacy.

The AAIS definition of personal injury is essentially the same as the ISO definition, except that the wording "in any manner" is added. Thus, "oral or written publication" becomes "oral or written publication, in any manner…". The MSO definition states that personal injury "means injury, other than *bodily injury*" so as to leave no doubt as to what is intended. However, a difference that might pose a problem in interpretation is that for wrongful entry and the like. The MSO definition for this injury is "wrongful entry into, or eviction of a person from, or invasion of the right of private occupancy of, a dwelling, room, or other private premises that the person occupies." Note the omission of the wording "committed by on or on behalf of its owner, landlord or lessor." It would almost appear that anyone intentionally entering a premises without reasonable cause to be there could be afforded umbrella coverage.

The MSO umbrella adds a definition that could be seen to apply to personal injury, and that is for *electronic aggression*:

Electronic aggression means harassment or bullying done by way of any type of electronic means *including*, but not limited to: blogs, chat rooms, email, instant messaging, social networking or text messaging.

This is not to say that ISO and AAIS do not address this topic; they do, but only through exclusionary language, while MSO adds a definition and then excludes coverage.

"Personal Injury" and the Courts

Determining the scope of "personal injury" coverage has proven almost as vexatious for the courts as deciding whether bodily injury and mental injury are linked. The problem, as evidenced in the cases discussed below, is how much the coverage is bounded by the exclusion (discussed in Chapter 6) for intentionally harmful acts. For example, since "malice" is defined in *Webster's Collegiate Dictionary (Tenth Edition)* as "desire to cause pain, injury, or distress to another," how can one commit *unintentional* "malicious prosecution"?

Although malicious prosecution cases are rare, they do happen. *Black's Law Dictionary (Eighth Edition)* defines *malicious prosecution* as "the institution of a criminal or civil proceeding for an improper purpose and without probable cause. The tort requires an adversary to prove four elements: (1) the initiation or continuation of a lawsuit; (2) lack of probable cause; (3) malice; and (4) favorable termination of the lawsuit." In other words, Party A sues Party B for slander, and the case is resolved in Party A's favor. Party B cannot then sue for malicious prosecution, since the outcome of the underlying suit had a termination favorable to party A.

We should note that there are few cases involving this situation. One that involved a case of neighbor *versus* neighbor was *Turnage v. Kasper*, 704 S.E.2d 842 (Ga. App. 2010). At one time the two families were friends, but the friendship ended acrimoniously. Turnage and other neighbors blocked Kasper and her son while they were riding their motorbikes, took Kasper's son's football and destroyed it, etc. Kasper was not, however, an angel turning the other cheek; there was evidence that she loudly confronted and shoved Turnage. The police were called on several occasions. Turnage demanded that the police arrest Kasper on battery charges, and issue a warrant to her to stay away from him. This was done. However, Kasper daily walked to the school bus stop to meet her children. Turnage and another man blocked her way, took her picture, and called the police, claiming Kasper had violated the warrant. Kasper was in jail about two weeks. Upon her release, she sued Turnage for malicious prosecution and intentional infliction of emotional distress.

The defendants—Turnage and other neighbors—claimed the police action meant they were not liable for malicious prosecution. But the court found the first arrest was not supported by probable cause, so the police actions did not hinder Turnage's liability. The court said several factors supported the malicious prosecution action: Turnage urged a law enforcement officer to begin criminal proceedings, and he provided information to the officer that he knew to be false. So, Turnage was guilty of malicious prosecution.

We saw that the AAIS and ISO definitions for personal injury included the wording that oral or written publication, *in any manner*, of material that slanders or libels a person's or organization's goods, products or services is included. As we will see later in the exclusions for personal injury, publication of that material with the knowledge that the material is false is not covered. A recent case proves that publication on the internet may also fall within the exclusion. *Caveat*, the internet is not open-range with no consequences. In the case of *Giustibelli v. Blake et al.*, 2016 WL 75000 (4th Fla. 2016) Blake and her husband were undergoing a divorce. Blake retained Giustibelli, but apparently the arrangement did not work out. Blake and her husband took to the internet to post "reviews," which stated, among other things, that Giustibelli was "combative and explosive" and took the divorce to "a level of anger which caused major suffering of my minor children… She insisted I was an emotionally abused wife who couldn't make rational decisions which caused my case to drag on… so her FEES would multiply…" Blake continued much in the same vein, stating that the attorney had charged her four times the original estimate. Giustibelli filed a libel suit. At trial, Blake admitted she had not been charged four times the original fees, and, in fact, the originally quoted fees were the ones charged. The court awarded Giustibelli $350,000 in damages. Of course, Blake and her husband appealed, arguing that they had merely expressed an opinion.

Now, a true opinion cannot support a libel verdict. A true opinion cannot be proven false. For example, I might hold that the Seattle Seahawks are the most overrated team in the NFL. Now, that will lend itself to disagreement, but not to a lawsuit—it's my opinion. But, if somehow I stated "facts" that I knew to be false to prove my opinion, publishing it as truth, then that is another matter entirely. For example, if I publish "facts" to the effect that the Cincinnati Bengals management charges up to 30 percent more that comparable teams for comparable tickets, so that attendance falls at games, that is libel since I have knowingly published something I know to be false. And that is what happened in the Giustibelli case. Blake and her husband knew that "four times the original fee" was false, and yet published this in a public, on-line review. The other "opinions" expressed (such as "poor service," "horrible image") did not alter the factual statement which the defendants knew to be false. First moral of story: take to the free-range "on-line review" carefully! Second moral of story: in the umbrella form, as in all policies of insurance, be sure that what appears to be a coverage grant is not taken away by a later exclusion. We will look at other cases later when the personal injury exclusions are discussed.

Occurrence

The insuring agreements of many personal umbrella policies promise to pay damages the insured is legally obligated to pay for bodily injury or property damages arising out of an occurrence. What, therefore, is an *occurrence*? (The coverage for personal injury, as previously noted, is triggered by an offense committed during the policy period.)

"Occurrence" means an accident, including continuous or repeated exposure to substantially the same general harmful conditions, which results, during the policy period, in:

(1) "bodily injury"; or

(2) "property damage".

This definition is a familiar one; indeed, it appears in the ISO homeowners form as well as in the personal umbrella. The AAIS definition is substantially the same. The MSO form, however, differs:

Occurrence means an accident, including continuous or repeated exposure to substantially the same general harmful conditions, or an offense listed in the definition of *personal injury*.

Occurrence does not include actual or alleged misrepresentation or omissions of any kind in the sale of real or personal property.

Remember the case of *Lowell K. Wood v. Safeco Insurance Company of America*, 980 S.W.2d 43 (Missouri 1998), where the question revolved around whether negligent misrepresentation was an accident, and therefore within the scope of an "occurrence" for coverage purposes (the details of the case were given in Chapter 1). The Missouri appellate court looked to Maryland in finding for the insured, quoting with approval the finding in *Sheets v. Brethren Mutual Ins. Co.*, 679 A.2d 540 (Maryland 1996): "If we were to adopt an objective standard and hold that the term 'accident' as used in liability insurance policies excludes coverage for damage that should have been foreseen or expected by the insured, such insurance policies would be rendered all but meaningless. Under such an interpretation, the policy would provide no coverage for negligent acts resulting in objectively foreseeable or expectable damage. Only acts of negligence resulting in objectively unforeseeable or unexpectable [sic] damage would be covered. Of course, under basic principles of tort law, the insured is unlikely to be held liable for unforeseeable or unexpectable [sic] damages resulting from his negligence. Thus, interpreting 'accident' as encompassing only negligent acts resulting in unforeseeable and unexpected damages would leave the insured covered against only those damages for which he or she is not likely to be held liable. We decline to adopt such a restrictive construction of the term accident." Had the definition of *occurrence* been that of the MSO form, clearly the court would not have held for the insured.

Earlier we mentioned the case of *Heacker v. Safeco Insurance Company of America*, *et al.*, 676 F.3d 724 (U.S. 8th 2012) in our discussion of bodily injury and mental injury. Heacker sued Jessica Wright and her insurers for equitable garnishment to collect a state court judgment. Wright had hacked into Heacker's email, Facebook, and voicemail, and continued to send anonymous texts and calls to harass and defame him for a period of nearly five years. Wright's children also participated in the harassment. Wright even went so far as to use a voice alteration service to make threatening calls. Heacker reached a settlement with one of Wright's insurers; this action ensued in an equitable garnishment action to collect $5 million in punitive damages. The court looked at the definition of "occurrence"—"an accident"—and stated it was up to Haecker to demonstrate that Wright's actions were accidental. Since they were not, the insurers were not responsible for the equitable garnishment.

Business

For the most, the personal umbrella is not intended to cover activities associated with an insured's business. (Business-related exclusions and exceptions will be examined in Chapter 6.) Look at the following MSO definition:

> *Business* means any occupation, profession, trade or commercial activity, including childcare activities undertaken for a fee or other payment.

The definition goes on to state that if form MPL 101 is listed in the Declarations, business does not include farming activities. For our purposes, we will use the basic definition. Now, contrast the MSO definition with the AAIS:

"Business" means:

a. a trade, a profession, or an occupation, including farming, all whether full time, part time, or occasional. This includes the leasing or rental of property to others; or

b. any other activity undertaken for money or other compensation, but this does not include:

   1) providing care services to a relative of an "insured";

   2) providing services for the care of persons who are not relatives of an "insured" for which the only compensation is the mutual exchange of like services;

   3) a volunteer activity for which:

      a) an "insured" receives no compensation; or

      b) an "insured's only compensation is the reimbursement of expenses incurred to carry out the activity; or

   4) an activity not described in 1) through 3) above for which no "insured's" total compensation for the 12 month period just before the first day of this policy period was more than $2,500.

The ISO definition is similar to the AAIS definition; however, the amount of money that can be received by an insured is $2,000. When we look at exclusions pertaining to business activities, we will see that certain individuals and activities are exempt from exclusionary language.

Motor Vehicles

The final definition to consider is "motor vehicle." At this point, we will only examine the different definitions; in Chapter 4 we will look at who is insured for use of a motor vehicle, what is excluded, etc. There is one common element: in the forms examined, motorized vehicles designed to assist the handicapped and motorized vehicles used to service a residence premises are not addressed. Since the underlying homeowners forms give coverage to such vehicles, there is no need. For a discussion of the liability coverage under the ISO, AAIS, and MSO homeowners policies, please see *Homeowners Coverage Guide, Fifth Edition* (August, 2014). We should perhaps note, though, that the current MSO homeowners form states that only "vehicles used solely to service an 'insured's residence" are given liability coverage—a wording that ISO changed from its 2000 to its 2011 form to reflect that such a vehicle might be used, for example, to mow an insured's aging parents' lawn.

We will first look at the MSO definition:

Motor vehicle means any self-propelled land vehicle, semi-trailer or trailer including any equipment or machinery attached to such.

This definition is extremely broad and could encompass almost any sort of vehicle. It is therefore only through exclusions that the umbrella policy is formed so as not to provide unintended coverage.

The AAIS form defines a "motorized vehicle":

a. a self-propelled land or amphibious vehicle, regardless of method of surface contact, but this does not include a:

   1) "hovercraft";

   2) model hovercraft that is not designed to carry people or cargo:

   3) "watercraft"; or

   4) model watercraft that is not designed or used to carry people or cargo; or

b. a trailer or semitrailer that:

   1) is attached to or being carried on or towed by; or

2) becomes detached while being carried on or towed by;

a. vehicle described in a. above.

In the AAIS form, a "hovercraft" means a "self-propelled motorized ground effect machine or air cushion vehicle designed or used to travel over land or water. This includes, but is not limited to, a flarecraft." A "ground effect" vehicle is one that travels on a self-generated cushion of air. Flarecraft may travel some four or five feet above the ground or water but usually no more than one and a half times wing span. The term does not include a model hovercraft not designed to carry persons or cargo.

The AAIS form also defines an "aircraft" as: "an apparatus or a device designed or used for flight, but this does not include a model aircraft not designed to carry people or cargo; a 'hovercraft'; or a model hovercraft that is not designed or used to carry people or cargo." The MSO form's definition of "aircraft" is similar: "any contrivance used or designed for flight, but does not include model or hobby craft unless used or designated to carry cargo or persons." At present, personally-owned drones could fall into the hobby category, but because of developments and emerging regulations this may change in the future. Is a drone carrying a camera carrying cargo? This needs to be sorted out.

The AAIS form's definition of "watercraft" is:

> ...an apparatus or a device primarily designed to be propelled on or in water by engine, motor, or wind, but this does not include:
>
> a. a model watercraft that is not designed or used to carry people or cargo;
>
> b. a "hovercraft";
>
> c. a model hovercraft that is not designed or used to carry people or cargo;
>
> d. a "motorized vehicle";
>
> e. an "aircraft"; or
>
> f. a model aircraft that is not designed or used to carry people or cargo.

"Watercraft" is not a defined term in the MSO umbrella. Indeed, the definitions of "watercraft" in both the AAIS and ISO forms are sufficiently vague so as to allow for coverage provided (with insurer approval) by underlying policies. For example, in the AAIS homeowner form liability attaches to a watercraft that is in storage, is a sailing vessel less that twenty-six feet in length, twenty-five or less horsepower outboard, etc. But in the umbrella, a "watercraft" simply means "an apparatus or a device primarily designed to be propelled on or in water by engine, motor, or wind…" The ISO umbrella definition is similar.

The ISO form does not refer to a motorized vehicle. Rather, there are two categories of motor vehicles. First, an "auto."

> "Auto" means:
>
> 1. A private passenger motor vehicle, motorcycle, moped or motor home;
> 2. A vehicle designed to be pulled by a private passenger motor vehicle or motor home; or
> 3. A farm wagon or farm implement while towed by a private passenger motor vehicle or motor home.

Note that the umbrella definition does not make the distinctions that, say, the PAP does. For example, under "newly acquired auto" in the PAP this means a "private passenger auto; or pickup or van…" This is because much of the umbrella coverage responds after underlying policy limits have been exhausted, and so the umbrella insurer will look at the underlying policy to make sure any vehicle in question has already been given liability coverage in the underlying policy. Also, the ISO definition will cover a farm wagon or implement while towed by a private passenger motor vehicle or motor home, but the definition does not encompass a farm tractor while being driven along the road. Remember that farming operations are not eligible under the ISO program. However, if a tractor is viewed as a vehicle not licensed for road use and used to service the premises, then coverage attaches through the homeowners.

Second, the ISO umbrella defines a recreational vehicle:

> "Recreational motor vehicle" means:
>
> 1. All-terrain vehicle;
> 2. Dune buggy;
> 3. Snowmobile; or
> 4. Any other motorized land vehicle which is designed for recreational use off public roads.

Remember that just defining a word or term does not mean that there will necessarily be coverage. However, when one has a grasp of the definitions, then finding coverage—or an exclusion—becomes much simpler.

In the next chapter, we will look at who is an insured.

Chapter 3

Who Is an Insured?

Introduction

As noted previously, the chief reason to purchase a personal umbrella policy is to protect one's assets. Personal umbrella policies promise to pay damages for which an insured becomes legally liable in event of a covered occurrence. Therefore, knowing who will be covered in event of a loss is vital. The following chapter will look at the wording used in different forms to describe an insured person, except for who is an insured for use of a motor vehicle or watercraft. These will be discussed in Chapters 4 and 5.

The prudent agent will regularly update information on umbrella insureds regarding who resides in the insured's home. Are there stepchildren? Is there shared custody? Do the insureds provide foster care?

The Named Insured and Spouse

In determining who is covered under any given umbrella for various activities, it is often necessary to look in different places in the policy. It is common to preface the definitions with wording such as this in the MSO form:

> *You, your* and *yourself* refer to the insured named in the Declarations.

In the AAIS form:

> The words "you" and "your" mean the person or persons named as the insured on the "declarations". This includes "your" spouse if a resident of "your" household.

The ISO form declares:

> Throughout this Policy, the words "you" and "your" refer to:
>
> 1. The "named insured" shown in the Declarations; and
> 2. The spouse if a resident of the same household.

Clarifying that coverage applies to the named insured and spouse if they reside in the same household avoids questions of coverage should the marriage terminate and one of the parties vacate the marital home. Without this provision, the insurer could conceivably provide liability coverage to two households for one premium.

A note of caution, though—the PAP (2005) states that:

> If the spouse ceases to be a resident of the same household during the policy period or prior to the inception of this policy, the spouse will be considered "you" and "your" under this policy but only until the earlier of:
>
> 1. The end of ninety days following the spouse's change of residency;
> 2. The effective date of another policy listing the spouse as a named insured; or
> 3. The end of the policy period.

Now, many insureds will have an underlying auto policy containing this or similar language. Therefore, an insured spouse could be in the untenable position of having underlying auto coverage but no umbrella coverage. Often when a marriage is ending the last person to be advised is the insurance agent. There is currently no such provision in any of the homeowners forms, nor in the umbrella forms.

It might be wise, in the event this situation occurs, to check with the underwriter to see if coverage can be extended until a separate umbrella policy is in place.

According to *Black's Law Dictionary, Eighth Edition*, a "spouse" is "one's wife or husband by lawful marriage." Currently, umbrella forms do not address other relationships between adults. Two unmarried adults who are desirous of umbrella coverage and who share living arrangements would each have to be shown as named insureds, if the insurer's underwriting practices permit. Of course, the ISO, the AAIS, and the MSO homeowners forms all allow liability (and property) coverage to be added for other household residents who are not spouses. The ISO form is HO 04 58, other residents of your household; the AAIS form is HO 6033, other residents of your household; and the MSO is MPL 40 companion coverage sections I and II. But again, these endorsements apply only to the underlying homeowners policy and not the umbrella. The AAIS form, as we will see in the section "Family Members as Insureds—Who are They?" includes a nonspouse, unrelated person as an insured by means of a definition of "household member"; this is the only form to do so. However, the term "household member" is used only in an exclusion for bodily injury to a household member, so this is perhaps insignificant. Also, in the AAIS form, a person granted "insured" status in underlying insurance is an insured with regard to the umbrella.

The Named Insured as a Trust

Often affluent families will place their assets—home, autos, watercraft, stocks, bonds, etc.—into a trust for their benefit during their lifetime. Current estimates are that about 20 percent of households do this. Now, there are ways to address the homeowners exposure. ISO has endorsement HO 06 15 05 11 trust endorsement; AAIS has two: HO 6072 provides coverages A, B, C, L, and M, while endorsement HO 6041 provides coverages A, B, L, and M. The MSO endorsement is MPL 23 residence held in trust. These endorsements are intended to provide liability coverage for occurrences arising out of the residence premises. With regard to auto coverage, the PAP has endorsement PP 13 03 trust endorsement. The vehicle's title must be held by the trust.

With regard to the personal umbrella, things become a bit more complicated. ISO has endorsement DL 99 09 02 15, on which the trust may be scheduled, and AAIS has endorsement PU 16 01 09 14 personal umbrella liability coverage expanded definition of insured. Now, this endorsement does not specifically state it may be used for a trust, but the endorsement does state that "'insured' means all persons *or entities* [italics added] granted status as an insured in 'underlying insurance', but only to the extent such status is granted in such 'underlying insurance'." Surely, a trust would qualify as *an entity*. The MSO program has endorsement MPL 23 residence held in trust sections I and II for its homeowners forms; however, there does not appear to be a specific endorsement which will allow the trust to be given coverage under the umbrella form. This might be a situation where the insurer manuscripts an endorsement to provide coverage.

Family Members as Insureds – Who Are They?

Having determined that the named insured and spouse are the "you" referred to before the definitions, the next place to see who is granted "insured" status is in the definitions themselves. Although this might seem fairly straightforward, definitions vary in the three forms we are discussing. Both AAIS and ISO define "insured," but then go on to further define terms used within that definition—for example, "insured" means a "relative" etc. "Relative" is not defined, but a relative is commonly held to be someone related by marriage, blood, or adoption.

The MSO form is perhaps the least complicated of the three forms. (Although brevity might be the soul of wit, it is not necessarily the soul of an insurance contract. Too few words may lead to too much unintended coverage.) The MSO form states that:

Insured means:

1. *You* and the following if residents of your household:
    - A. *Your* spouse.
    - B. *Your* or *your* spouse's relatives.
    - C. Anyone under the age of 21 in *your* care or the care of a resident relative.
2. A full time student, as defined by the school, who was a resident of *your* household before moving out to attend school, provided that such student is under the age of:
    - A. 24 and is *your* or *your* spouse's relative, or
    - B. 21 and in *your* care or that of a resident relative.
3. Any other persons with respect to their liability because of acts of an *insured* described in the preceding Paragraphs 1 and 2.

Definition 3 might lead one to believe that a personal injury such as wrongful imprisonment committed by an insured, with the help of a friend talked into the action, would give the friend insured status. Also, as has long been the case with the AAIS and ISO forms, whenever "an insured" is mentioned, the term is intended to include "one or more insureds." That would not appear to be the case with the MSO form.

The next definitions we will examine are those in the AAIS form. The place to begin is with *insured*:

Except as stated within this definition, "insured" means all persons or entities granted status as an insured in "underlying insurance", but only to the extent such status is granted in such "underlying insurance."

No person is an "insured" with respect to the use of a "motorized vehicle" or "watercraft" unless that person has a reasonable expectation that he or she has a right to such use. However, this does not apply to the use of a "motorized vehicle" or "watercraft" that "you" own, or a "motorized vehicle" that "you" lease under a written agreement for a continuous period of at least six months, by a person who is:

a. "your" relative and a resident of "your" household;

b. "your" relative under the age of 25 years who:

1) is financially dependent upon "you";

2) is a student enrolled in school full time, as defined by the school; and

3) was a resident of "your" household just before moving out to attend school;

c. under the age of 21 years and who:

1) is not "your" relative;

2) resides in "your" household; and

3) is in "your" care or in the care of "your" resident relatives; or

d. under the age of 21 years and who:

1) is not "your" relative;

2) is in "your" care or in the care of "your" resident relatives;

3) is a student enrolled in school full time, as defined by the school; and

4) was a resident of "your" household just before moving out to attend school.

The phrase an "insured", wherever it appears in this policy, means one or more "insureds".

Note that the AAIS definition of "insured" encompasses not only the status of household residents and relatives, but also their use of a motor vehicle. The AAIS definition is broader than that of the MSO form in that a full-time student may be twenty-five years of age, although the student should be financially dependent on the named insured—not mentioned in the MSO form. We should add that the AAIS form also includes a definition of "household member," which is essentially the same as the definition of "insured," with one exception, and that is for "an 'insured', other than a person described in a. through d. [above], who: 1) lives with 'you'; 2) is a member of 'your' household; and 3) is not a guest, 'domestic employee', 'employee', tenant, or roomer or boarder…". We will discuss this in connection with the intrafamily exclusion later in the chapter (Un)Common Exclusions.

Finally, we turn to the ISO definition of "insured," which means:

1. You.

2. A "family member".

3. Any person using an "auto", "recreational motor vehicle", or watercraft, which is owned by you and covered under this Policy. Any person using a temporary substitute for such "auto" or "recreational motor vehicle" is also an "insured".

4. Any other person or organization but only with respect to the legal responsibility for acts or omissions of you or any "family member" while you or any "family member" is using an "auto" or "recreational motor vehicle" covered under this Policy. However, the owner or lessor of an "auto" or "recreational motor vehicle" loaned to or hired for use by an "insured" or an "insured's" behalf, is not an "insured".

5. With respect to animals owned by you or any "family member", any person or organization legally responsible for such animals. However, a person or organization using or having custody of such animals in the course of any "business" or without the consent of the owner is not an "insured".

Now, the definition of "family member":

"Family member" means a resident of your household who is:

1. Your relative, including a ward or foster child; or

2. Under the age of 21 and in the care of you or an "insured" who is age 21 or over.

Note that the ISO definition is much narrower than that of the AAIS form. In fact, it does not even recognize the possibility of a full-time student over age twenty-one but under twenty-four as does the ISO homeowners, and there is no endorsement available to add coverage. Neither is there any recognition of a household member who may be insured by endorsement (HO 04 58 05 11 other members of your household, for example), and the definition does not mention others who might be given "insured" status on underlying insurance. This omission could lead to a serious gap in coverage. In fact, it is similar to the definition found in the ISO homeowners HO 00 03 04 91, in which an "'insured' means you and residents of your household who are your relatives…" This definition led to much litigation over insured (or not) status for children who became full-time students—were they or were they not residents? Generally, in the case of full-time students, the courts found they were residents, since they were dependent upon their parents, returned to the parental home during breaks, etc. In fact, according to *9 Couch on Insurance* (§128:11) "One court has stated that, in light of the contemporary realities of family living, in which most students remain residents of their parents' houses long after the age of majority, it is incumbent upon insurance companies to state clearly that students are not covered if they are not physically living with their parents on the date of the accident so that the average purchaser of insurance understands this limitation in coverage." See *Fire Ins. Exchange v. Pring-Wilson*, 831 F. Supp. 2d 493 (D. Mass. 2011, applying Colorado law).

What Is a Residence?

There are three common situations where the question of residency arises. The first of these is where a child attends a school or college and lives away from the parental home for much of the year. We have already looked at how a student is insured (or not) in our discussion of the definition of family member insureds. The second situation involves relatives in an assisted living facility. Third, we will discuss children of divorce.

Relative in an Assisted Living Facility

A relative in an assisted living facility may be given coverage—both property and liability—in the ISO, AAIS, and MSO homeowners programs. The respective endorsements are: HO 04 59, HO 6235, and MPL 143. These are attached to the homeowners policy, and a relative of an insured is then scheduled, along with the location of the facility. Note that even though these individuals are relatives of the named insured's, they are not, nor may they necessarily ever have been, residents of the named insured's household. Rather, these endorsements provide an easy way for a concerned relative to be sure a relative in such a facility has proper insurance. No auto coverage is available.

However, at present, only the ISO program has an umbrella endorsement specifically targeted at the relative. It is DL 98 07 02 15. The endorsement will not take the place of underlying insurance; in fact, it states that underlying coverage must be in place. (We should note that the ISO endorsement HO 04 59 does not specifically state that the person scheduled is an "insured." Rather, the endorsement states that the insurer agrees to insure the person, and extends liability coverage with some exclusions. It might be left to a court of law to determine whether this constitutes *insured* status.) The AAIS program has endorsement PU 1601 09 14 expanded definition of insured, which presumably could be used. This endorsement states that "'insured' means all persons or entities granted status as an insured in 'underlying insurance' but only to the extent such status is granted in such 'underlying insurance'." Again, as with the ISO program, the relative is not designated as an "insured" in the endorsement, so should a question arise it might have to be answered in a court of law.

Children of Divorce

We have noted that the question of a child's residence can be a difficult one to answer. According to *8 Couch on Insurance* (§ 114:21) "Special problems arise in connection with children of divorced or separated parents, one of whom is the named insured. The matter frequently is determined on the basis of which parent has primary custody of the children. However, when joint custody is involved, legal custody may not be dispositive of the issue. Similarly, where the parents do not view a legal custody in one parent as meaning that the child resides exclusively with that parent, then some weight may be given to the parents' interpretation of their children's residence situation." Many courts take into account extrinsic evidence as to a child's residence, for example: where has the child spent regular time? If living with one parent, is there an expectation that the child will return to the home of the other parent? Are there close ties of kinship? Does the child enjoy all the living facilities of the home? Some courts hold that the intent of the parents, and not the child, regarding residence is what determines the case. But when there is joint custody, it is possible for a child to reside with both parents as a matter of law. For example, in the case of *Nationwide Ins. Co. v. Alli*, 896 N.E.2s 732 (Oh. App. 3d 2008) the court said "The phrase 'resident of your household' in a policy of insurance includes the children of divorced parents who live consistently with their nonresidential parent." See, also the case of *Dusham v. Nationwide Ins. Co.*, 92 F. Supp. 2d 353 (D. Vt. 2000) in which the daughter of divorced parents resided primarily with her father. However, the court found she was also a relative, and therefore an insured, under her mother's automobile policy. The policy defined a *relative* as "one who regularly lives in your household, related to you by blood." The daughter lived with her mother at least two weekends per month.

In another considerably older, but nonetheless valid, California case, the court found that the named insured's comprehensive liability policy provided coverage for his six-year-old son, who was staying with his mother. The mother was separated from her husband at the time. The situation was complicated by two custody decrees—the first provided for divided custody, and the second for custody in the mother with rights of visitation by the father. The child had been living with his father, and the accident happened a few days after he left to live a time with his mother. The mother stated she had not interpreted the modified decree as meaning that the boy's residence was to be exclusively with her. See *Cal-Farm Ins. Co. v. Boisseranc*, 312 P.2d 401 (1st. Dist. 1957).

The bottom line, in situations involving a divorce, keep all the children's living arrangements on record, if at all possible.

Status of a Ward or Foster Child

The wording of personal umbrella policies, as well as underlying homeowners and auto policies, makes it clear that, for coverage purposes, wards and foster children are accorded "insured" status. Therefore, if a ward or foster child in the named insured's custody were to negligently injure someone – say, cause another child at school to trip and fall down a flight of stairs – there would be coverage. But the "down side" to this is that because of the ward's or foster child's status as an insured, should the ward or foster child become injured because of the named insured's negligence, and a suit be brought against the named insured claiming damages for the child, there is no coverage for the named insured because of the intrafamily exclusion.

Generally, in the case of foster children, there is no question as to their status. But when does the foster child cease to be a foster child? A recent Pennsylvania case tried to address this. In *Rourke v. Penn. National Mutual Cas. Ins. Co*, 116A 3d 87 (Pa. Super. 2015), the foster child of the insured was injured while riding with a friend. The friend's policy paid its limits but there were still injuries to the child. However, the "child" in this case was nineteen and had been terminated by youth services at age eighteen. The boy continued to live with his foster parents as he had for the past six and a half years. In finding for the insured the court said that he could well be considered a "ward" of the Rourkes, and said that the familial bonds in place would indicate the strong relationship necessary to consider him a part of the family. We should add that the day of the accident the Rourkes added the young man to their auto policy as a driver; however, that did not appear to influence the judge's decision.

But in the case of *Glen Falls Insurance Company v. Smith et al.*, 617 S.E.2d 760 (W.Va. 2005) the court was not inclined to be lenient. Here, the claimant was injured as a passenger in a single-car accident. The driver's policy limits were insufficient for the claimant's injuries. So, he turned to his mother's auto policy's underinsured coverage. He did not reside with his mother, though, but with his mother's divorced husband (who was not the claimant's biological father). So, he turned to that person's auto policy, stating that he thought of him as a father and that he was his ward. The court held that a legal arrangement was necessary to establish that bond, and since the claimant was over age twenty-one and held a job, the fact that he resided with a man whom he called "dad" did not make for coverage.

If any insureds care for foster children, they should make sure the agency placing the children has coverage in place that would protect the insureds should such a need arise.

Adult "Children"

There is a comedic standard about adult "children" residing in the basements of their parents' homes. Unfortunately, many of the parents involved are groaning rather than laughing. Be that as it may, thc status of these "children" has implications with regard to their coverage. We will take a look at situations involving not only single adults, but adults who have married, have children, and have, for one reason or another, moved back with their parents. Although in the case of a young adult residing in the parental home the answer might be reasonably simple as to whether or not that person is a "resident relative" for coverage purposes, the answer is not nearly so clear-cut when there are essentially two households residing under one roof.

Before embarking on resident relatives, we look at one case involving roommates. A passenger who was injured in a vehicle driven by her roommate was not entitled to receive UM or liability coverage under the roommate's auto policy, since she was not a family member or a member of the insured's household. The court found that the relationship was purely economic, and that there was no indication of a household (see *Shivvers v. American Family Insurance Co., et al.*, 589 N.W. 2d 129 [Neb. 1999]).

In the case of *Fire Ins. Exchange v. Pring-Wilson*, 831 F. Supp. 2d 493 (D. Mass 2011) the court applied Colorado law and found that the insured's adult son (a second-year graduate student) was "living with her" within the meaning of the umbrella policy, even though he had temporary addresses while at school, since her residence would have continued to be his for the foreseeable future. The young man was attacked while walking down the street, and drew a knife from his backpack to defend himself. One of his assailants, who didn't realize he'd been stabbed, later died, and so the student was sued for wrongful death. The court found the student was entitled to coverage under his mother's homeowners and umbrella policies as an insured.

But in the case of *Berryhill v. Entergy New Orleans Inc. et al.*, 925 So. 2d 12 (LA App. 2006) when James Berryhill was determined to be a resident of his mother's house the finding did not work to his advantage, since he had sued his mother for injuries sustained when he attempted to light a gas space heater in order to take a bath. The court said that "'residency' is a matter of intention and choice, and not necessarily physical location." James lived with his girlfriend, and on the day in question had gone to his mother's home to bathe since there was no hot water at his girlfriend's house. The court reviewed much evidence, including the facts that James used his mother's address on medical records, job applications, unemployment compensation, and state ID card. He also kept personal belongings at his mother's and received mail there, and had moved back after other relationships had ended. So, as an insured, he had no status to sue.

The victim of a dog bite brought suit against the dog's owner and his mother for her injury, which occurred when the owner was visiting his mother. The dog's owner primarily lived in his home in Massachusetts rather than in his mother's home in New Hampshire, and considered himself a resident of Massachusetts. Apparently he kept his New Hampshire driver's license and voter registration because of inertia, rather than any ties to the state in which his mother lived. Thus, he was not an adult "resident relative" and therefore not entitled to insured status. This case is *White v. Vermont Mutual Insurance Company*, 106 A.3d 1159 (N.H. 2014).

Finally, we look at the case of *Farmers Mutual Insurance Company v. Tucker et al.,* 576 S.E. 2d 261 (W. Va. 2002). Here, the homeowners liability insurer brought action against the victim for a declaratory judgment that the named insured's adult child, who lived in a mobile home on the named insured's property, was not an insured when he threw hot grease out the door of the mobile home and seriously injured another person. (The other person spotted smoke coming from the mobile home, and went to the door to help just at the moment the adult son was opening the door to throw the smoking grease out.) The supreme court of appeals held that the phrase "resident of your household" could mean a "person who dwells, though not necessarily under a common roof, with other individuals who are named insureds in a manner and for a sufficient length of time so that they could be considered to be a family living together." The named insured's son lived in a mobile home on the insured's property, gave his identifying address as their address, and received financial help from them. His mother also shopped for him and he frequently ate meals with his parents. Therefore, he was entitled to be covered as an insured. We should add, though, that there were two dissenting opinions.

Married, with (Married) Children

The next situation to be discussed is what happens, as is often the case, when married children (and their families) return to the parental home following, say, a corporate down-sizing. As was the case with unmarried children such as those discussed above, when the facts would seem to warrant agreement, the courts in the cases discussed below reach completely different conclusions.

The Tischhausers' daughter and her husband and children (the Clevelands) arrived at the Tischhausers' mobile home to stay until the husband could find work. During the time the Clevelands had been married, they stayed temporarily with the Tischhausers a number of times when they were having financial difficulties.

On this occasion, they arrived at the Tischhausers' mobile home with their belongings in a trailer. They unloaded their belongings and placed them in a garage on the premises, where they remained, except for some clothing, for the next several weeks. After unpacking the trailer, James Cleveland and the Tischhausers left to return the trailer. During the time they were gone, Douglas, one of the Cleveland children, started a fire that destroyed the mobile home and its contents, as well as property of a neighbor. The Tischhausers' carrier denied coverage for Douglas, holding that he was not an insured, and the neighbors sued their carrier. The trial court found, and the Oregon court of appeals affirmed, that the Clevelands were temporary guests of the Tischhausers, and not members of their household. Said the court in *Guenther H. Lang et al. v. Foremost Insurance Company*, 778 P.2d 510 (Oregon 1989), "The evidence permits the conclusion that, although the Clevelands' stay was to be of an indefinite length, it was not to be permanent and that the Clevelands were only financially dependent (the Tischhausers paid the Clevelands' living expenses) until James found employment. The evidence also supports a finding that the Clevelands and the Tischhausers were separate family units."

Now, a look at a case that reached the opposite conclusion to *Lang*, above, with facts that are remarkably similar. The case is *Arden B. Engerbretsen et al. v. Arden A. Engerbretsen, et al.*, 675 A.2d 13 (Delaware 1995). Arden B. Engerbretsen and his wife were insured by United Services Auto Association (USAA) under homeowners and personal umbrella policies. Their son, Arden A Engerbretsen, his wife, and their two children were staying with them while he looked for employment. They arrived there in March of 1990 and intended to leave by November 5th, either for a hoped-for job in New York or to move to Arizona.

However, on November 2, 1990, Arden A. Engerbretsen was using a tractor-mower owned by his parents (Arden B.) to mow the lawn behind their house. Unbeknownst to him, his son Andrew, age two, was nearby. He backed the mower and accidentally knocked Andrew down and ran over him. A claim was submitted, and USAA extended coverage under the homeowners section F medical payments to others. The insurer denied coverage under the liability portion, however, citing the exclusion of coverage for bodily injury to an insured. (USAA later asserted that payment under medical payments did not constitute a waiver of the exclusionary provision of coverage E liability.)

The superior court considered the meaning of "residents of the [named insured's] household" since this term was not defined in the homeowners policy. "The main disagreement among the courts relates to whether, in determining the meaning of the term, the subjective intentions of the occupier and the policyholder as to the transient or permanent nature of the stay should be considered. In other words, the dispute involves whether the temporal element of the stay at the policyholder's premises is relevant to the analysis," stated the court, noting that both plaintiffs and defendants brought several cases to prove their point.

One of the cases pointed to by the defendants (Arden A.) was *Lang*, discussed above. As noted earlier, the two cases are remarkably similar. But the court in *Engerbretsen*, although noting the similarity, said "there are other factors to consider which may overcome the stated intent of a transitory living arrangement... The circumstances in this case go beyond a mere temporary living arrangement while the father looked for employment... In the court's view, the record establishes a portrait of a close, extended family, living as members of a single household under one roof for a substantial period of time, sharing meals and vacationing together. The court is convinced that the circumstances in this case... outweigh the declared subjective intention of defendants of a temporary living arrangement. Thus, the court concludes that defendants were residents of the grandparents' household under the policy on the date of Andrew's accident." Therefore, the court held the defendants were residents and so fell within the injury to an insured exclusion of coverage E. Coverage was precluded. It should be noted that the question of whether USAA's payment under coverage F medical payments to others constituted a waiver of their right to deny coverage under coverage E was not addressed.

Finally, in *Reed v. American Standard Insurance Company of Wisconsin*, 231 S.W.3d 851 (Mo. App. 2007), the father of children killed in an auto accident brought wrongful death action against the auto insurer of the children's uncle, seeking UM benefits on the claim that they were relatives living in the uncle's household and covered under his auto policy. But the court found they were not members of the uncle's household: they lived with their mother and her fiancé in a basement apartment of the uncle's house. The policy defined a relative as "a person related to the insured and living in the insured's household." Thus, although the children were related to their uncle, they were not living in his household.

Whenever there is a doubt or question as to who will be considered a resident relative for coverage (or exclusionary) purposes, it may be prudent to review case law in any given jurisdiction. Remember that not only is a resident's status important with regard to him or her being considered an insured for liability purposes, but also with regard to the exclusion for bodily injury to an insured, which we will discuss in Chapter 6.

Chapter 4

Motor Vehicles

Introduction

There are steps to take in determining whether or not coverage is provided or excluded with regard to the use of a motor vehicle. First, check the definition to see what any given insurer considers a "motor vehicle." Then consider "who is an insured" for use of a particular vehicle. Finally, examine the exclusions. This chapter primarily looks at coverage for motor vehicles, private passenger motor vehicles in particular. Recreational motor vehicles will be discussed in Chapter 5.

The "Family Auto"

Because the reason many persons purchase a personal umbrella policy is to provide increased liability protection for damages arising from covered auto accidents, it is important to understand exactly who is an insured for use of the family's private passenger auto(s). As noted earlier, the ISO Personal Auto Policy (PAP), 2005 edition, extends coverage in event a spouse ceases to be a resident of the household for a period of the earlier of: (a) the end of ninety days following the spouse's change of residency; (b) the effective date of another policy listing the spouse as a named insured; or (c) the end of the policy period. Therefore, the spouse continues to be a named insured during this time, and so covered on the auto policy. However, as we have noted, there is currently no such provision in any of the umbrella forms reviewed.

Therefore, if this situation arises, contact the insurer to see if arrangement can be made to extend the umbrella coverage similarly until other coverage can be arranged.

Motor Vehicles Defined

Before continuing our discussion of coverages and exclusions for motor vehicles in the umbrella form, we take a quick look at what a motor (or motorized) vehicle is. First, in the MSO form, a *motor vehicle* means "any self-propelled land vehicle, semi-trailer or trailer including any equipment or machinery attached to such." The ISO form does not define a motor vehicle, but rather an *auto*: "1. A private passenger motor vehicle, motorcycle, moped or motor home; 2. A vehicle designed to be pulled by a private passenger motor vehicle or motor home; or 3. A farm wagon or farm implement while towed by a private passenger motor vehicle or motor home." Finally, the AAIS form defines a *motorized vehicle*: "a. a self-propelled land or amphibious vehicle, regardless of method of surface contact… or b. a trailer or semitrailer that: 1) is attached to or being carried on or towed by; or 2) becomes detached while being carried on or towed by; a vehicle described in a. above." (Note that this is not the complete AAIS definition. For the complete definition, refer to Chapter 2 or to the policy form in the Appendices.)

"Insured" Defined

A personal umbrella should cover the named insured, spouse (if resident of the same household), and family members or resident relatives as defined. It is not uncommon for young persons, with their parents' consent, to have vehicles titled in their own names. Technically, these vehicles should be written on separate policies, since at that point for physical damages purposes the parents are presumed to have no insurable interest. Some insurers, however, will allow the vehicles to be added to the parents' policy.

If family members have their own auto policies, it is vital that the limits of coverage be in accordance with the umbrella insurer's requirements. The family members and their autos should be shown as insureds on an application or declarations.

Who, then, is considered an insured with regard to the use of a motor vehicle? First, we review the MSO definition of an *insured*:

Insured means:

1. *You* and the following if residents of your household:
   - A. *Your* spouse.
   - B. *Your* or *your* spouse's relatives.
   - C. Anyone under the age of 21 in *your* care or the care of a resident relative.
2. A full time student, as defined by the school, who was a resident of *your* household before moving out to attend school, provided that such student is under the age of:
   - A. 24 and is *your* or *your* spouse's relative; or
   - B. 21 and in *your* care or that of a resident relative.
3. Any other persons with respect to their liability because of acts of an insured described in the preceding Paragraphs 1 and 2.

This definition applies to those who will be considered "insured" for use of a motor vehicle. As we will see, it is extremely narrow and conceivably could lead to disputes over coverage. Remember, MSO has no personal auto policy and it is likely that many persons will have the ISO PAP as their underlying auto form. So, a person granted "insured" status under the PAP might have to determine whether the PAP coverage grant extends in line with the MSO umbrella.

Next, the AAIS definition:

> "Except as stated within this definition, 'insured' means all persons or entities granted status as an insured in 'underlying insurance', but only to the extent such status is granted in such 'underlying insurance'.
>
> No person is an 'insured' with respect to the use of a 'motorized vehicle'… unless that person has a reasonable expectation that he or she has a right to such use. However, this does not apply to the use of a 'motorized vehicle'… that 'you' own, or a 'motorized vehicle' that 'you' lease under a written agreement for a continuous period of at least six months, by a person who is…" [The definition is given in its entirety in Chapter 3.]

Obviously, this definition with regards to who is an insured for the use of a motor vehicle is much broader than that in the MSO form. Now, AAIS does not have an auto form, but it appears that the AAIS form drafters have carefully considered the auto forms in common use.

Before continuing with the ISO definition, we look at "use of a motor vehicle." "Use" of a motor vehicle is rarely defined, and it should be noted that "use" need not equate with actual operation of the vehicle. For example, a passenger may be "using" a vehicle to provide personal transportation. The passenger could distract the driver, thus causing an accident. An elderly neighbor might ask another neighbor to run an errand for him; even though not actually driving he is still "using" the car. Therefore, the insuring language should address these situations. We will look at "permissive user" later in this chapter.

Now, the ISO definition of insured with regard to motor vehicle usage:

> "Insured means: [1. and 2. omitted]
>
> 3. Any person using an 'auto' … which is owned by you and covered under this Policy. Any person using a temporary substitute for such 'auto' … is also an 'insured'.
>
> 4. Any other person or organization but only with respect to the legal responsibility for acts or omissions of you or any 'family member' which you or any 'family member' is using

> an 'auto' ... covered under this Policy. However, the owner or lessor of an 'auto'... loaned to or hired for use by an 'insured' or on an 'insured's behalf, is not an 'insured'.

The ISO umbrella definition incorporates many of the ISO PAP policy's definitions. However, unlike the AAIS definition, it does not mention that a private passenger vehicle leased under a written agreement for a period of at least six months will be considered as owned by the insured; that is found in the PAP Definition C.

Organizations

The ISO personal auto policy (PAP) describes an "insured" as including "for 'your covered auto', any person or organization but only with respect to legal responsibility for acts or omissions of a person for whom coverage is afforded under this Part [the Insuring Agreement]."

The ISO umbrella form, therefore, says an insured means "any other person or organization but only with respect to the legal responsibility for acts or omissions of you or any 'family member'..." So, for example, an insured might be using her car to help deliver Girl Scout cookies. If she negligently runs into another vehicle at an intersection and the other driver sues both the insured and the Girl Scout Council, the Council is an insured. An "organization" need not be not for profit; it might be a business, which, if legally responsible for an insured's use of an auto, is also an insured.

In the MSO umbrella form, there is no specific mention of persons or organizations being covered with respect to an insured's use of a motor vehicle. The pertinent wording is found as an exception to the aircraft, motor vehicles, and watercraft exclusion. After stating that the insurer will not cover any bodily injury, property damage, or personal injury arising out of maintenance, operation, ownership, or use of any aircraft, motor vehicle, or watercraft owned or operated by, or rented to or loaned to, any insured, the exception says "This exclusion... does not apply to the extent that coverage for such is provided in underlying primary insurance."

In the AAIS form, though, "all persons or entities granted status as an insured in 'underlying insurance'" are considered insureds. If the underlying auto policy is the ISO PAP (or a form utilizing the ISO language) the organization is granted coverage as an insured on the auto policy (see definition above).

However, there are two things to be aware of regarding this coverage provision. First, no matter how many persons or organizations seek coverage for a claim arising out of one occurrence, the limits will not be increased. Second, not all auto policies – particularly the nonstandard ones – cover anyone other than the named insured. Many umbrella insurers, for this reason among others, are hesitant to write an umbrella policy over a nonstandard auto policy.

If this coverage provision is important – if an insured, say, does much driving for a charitable organization, or even occasionally drives the charity's clients – then consider increasing the umbrella limits. Remember, limits are not increased, no matter how many claims arise out of an occurrence. It might also be prudent to see how the charity's own insurance would respond to the volunteer's use of his or her vehicle.

Legal Representatives

There is another class of insured with regards to motor vehicles, and that is the insured's legal representative(s). The legal representative is someone acting on behalf of a deceased, such as the executor of a will. This provision appears in different places depending upon the umbrella form reviewed; sometimes under "who is an insured" and other times in the conditions or general provisions. The MSO form covers legal representatives, and also someone having "proper" custody (for example, a thief cannot steal a deceased insured's vehicle and claim coverage under the umbrella should an accident occur):

> If *you* die, *your* rights and duties will be transferred to *your* legal representative but only while acting within the scope of duties as *your* legal representative. Until *your* legal representative is appointed, anyone having proper temporary custody of *your* property will have *your* rights and duties but only with respect to that property.

The AAIS form is quite explicit as to the transfer of an insured's rights in event of death:

> The "terms" in a. below apply if a person named as the insured on the "declarations" dies.
>
> a. The deceased person's rights and duties will be transferred to:
>
> 1) the surviving spouse, if a resident of the deceased person's household at the time of death;
>
> 2) the legal representative of the deceased person, but only:
>
> a) with respect to property of the deceased person that is covered by this policy at the time of death; and

b) while acting within the scope of duties as the deceased person's legal representative; or

3) anyone having proper, temporary custody of property of the deceased person that is covered by this policy at the time of death, but only with respect to such property and only until the deceased person's legal representative is appointed and qualified.

Finally, the ISO form. The ISO form says the policy will cover the surviving spouse if they are a resident in the same household at the time of death, and covers legal representatives:

c. The legal representative of the deceased person as if a named insured shown in the Declarations. This applies only with respect to the representative's legal responsibility to maintain or use your "autos" or the residence premises shown in the Declarations.

The ISO form is the only one to specifically mention a representative's legal responsibility to maintain or use the insured's "autos." The wording reflects the ISO PAP with regard to a legal representative's "legal responsibility to maintain or use 'your covered auto'." The wording of the AAIS and MSO umbrella forms, with their reference to the legal representative's *duties,* should still encompass use of the deceased's motor vehicles. Since a legal representative often arranges for a sale of property, he or she would normally want to make sure the vehicles being sold are in running order.

Permissive Users and the Reasonable Belief Wording

Questions of what constitutes permission are often vexatious. The ISO personal auto policy (2005 edition) excludes liability coverage for any insured "using a vehicle without a reasonable belief that that 'insured' is entitled to do so" (exclusion A.8.). However, the exception states that the exclusion "does not apply to a 'family member' using 'your covered auto' which is owned by you."

So, a family member using a vehicle owned by the named insured may be presumed to have permission to do so. (This saves the insurer from having to sort out cases of "But Mom, you TOLD me I could drive.") See, for example, the case of *United Services Automobile Association v. William Todd Dunn et al.*, 598 So. 2d 1169 (Louisiana 1992), where the appellate courts held that the language without the exception was ambiguous, and so resolved the suit in favor of the insured. James Timothy, a resident of his parents' household, allegedly struck two pedestrians. The auto and umbrella insurer, USAA, denied coverage, asserting that the young driver did not have his parents' permission to drive when the accident occurred. Everyone involved – pedestrians, driver, and insurer – filed suit for summary judgment.

The insurer held that the policy clearly and unambiguously excluded coverage for all persons using the covered auto without the named insured's consent. The trial court disagreed, and the appellate court, construing language like that above, affirmed that the ambiguity led to coverage. Stated the court, "when the coverage clause and the exclusion are read together, we see that coverage is provided to family members and to any person who uses a covered auto, except for any person who uses a covered auto who does not have a reasonable belief that he or she is entitled to use it. If the company had intended to exclude family members, it should have used the term 'covered person' in the exclusion because 'covered person' was defined to mean family members and any persons using covered autos. Because the exclusion does not apply to family members, coverage is afforded to family member James G. Timothy."

The permissive use theory may extend even beyond the original person given permission to use a vehicle. In *Federated Mutual Insurance Company v. Corey Davis et al.*, 919 F.Supp. 1001 (Mississippi 1995), the district court looked to the Mississippi supreme court's past resolution of issues relating to the coverage of a permissive user, and found no reason to deviate. The supreme court held that "[t]he 'general rule' that a permittee may not allow a third party to 'use' the named insured's car has generally been held not to preclude recovery under the omnibus clause where (1) the original permittee is riding in the car at the time of the accident, or (2) the second permittee, in using the vehicle is serving some purpose of the original permittee. The courts generally reason that under such circumstances the second permittee is 'operating' the car for the 'use of the first permittee' and that such 'use' is within the coverage of the omnibus clause." So, for example, if the named insured gives his son permission to drive his Lincoln Town Car to the prom, and the son consumes alcohol and allows a friend to take over the wheel, the friend is thus operating the vehicle for the purpose of keeping the son safe.

"Permissive use" can even venture into the realms of a rental car. In *Government Employees Insurance Company v. Hughes*, 921 N.E. 2d 269 (Oh. App. 2009), the court held that the named insured's auto policy provided liability coverage for the friend to whom she had loaned her auto. Her auto, at that point, happened to be a rental car and the insurer argued that the rental agency had not given the friend permission to drive. However, the named insured had rented the car while her own was in the shop for repairs, thus making the rental a temporary substitute. As such, the named insured could give permission for the friend to drive it.

Corporate Vehicles and Business Use

There are several considerations in regards to corporate vehicles. This next section looks at personal umbrella coverage for "company cars," corporately titled vehicles, and business use.

Company Cars

A common situation in many households is for one person to have a company car; that is, a vehicle regularly furnished for his use in connection with a business. (Situations where a business owner titles the family's personal passenger vehicles in the name of the business are considered separately; see below.) Often, the company car may be used for personal needs as well as for the business. The personal auto policy (PAP) does not provide liability coverage for an insured's use of any vehicle furnished or available for the named insured's regular use (exclusion B.2. precludes coverage for any vehicle, other than the insured's covered auto, that is furnished or available for the reguar use of the named insured). Therefore, if an insured has a regularly-furnished vehicle, care must be taken in determining how any given personal umbrella will treat this exposure.

Generally, if there is personal underlying auto coverage, then the personal umbrella will respond to a loss. So, if there is no personal auto policy in place, other arrangements must be made. The ISO personal auto policy, remember, precludes liability coverage:

> We do not provide liability coverage for the ownership, maintenance or use of…
>
> 2. Any vehicle, other than 'your covered auto', which is:
>   a. Owned by you; or
>   b. Furnished or available for your regular use.
> 3. Any vehicle, other than 'your covered auto', which is:
>   a. Owned by any 'family member'; or
>   b. Furnished or available for the regular use of any 'family member'.
>
> However, this exclusion (B.3.) does not apply to you while you are maintaining or 'occupying' any vehicle which is:
>
> a. Owned by a 'family member'; or
> b. Furnished or available for the regular use of a 'family member'.

Coverage gaps arise when the only auto in a household is a company-furnished vehicle and there is no personal auto policy in place. Or, there may be personal autos along with the business auto. Depending on the particular business auto policy in place, the company-car insured may not be covered for his or her use of any other vehicle.

Say, for example, husband and wife are both named insureds on a PAP. The wife has a company car. One day the husband's personal car is in the shop for repairs, but since his wife is out of town he takes the company car. While using his cell phone to call a customer he glances down at some papers, and negligently runs into the back of a legally stopped school bus. The family's personal auto policy will respond to this loss, since exclusion B.3.b. does not apply to "you"—the named insured—while occupying a vehicle regularly furnished to a family member. But what if a son drives a company car, and the daughter drives it and causes an accident. "She" is not "you." Or, perhaps the couple resides in New York City where they have no need for a personal car, relying on a company car for transportation, or renting a vehicle when they travel.

There are ways to plug these coverage gaps. First, in the case of a regularly furnished company car where there are personal vehicles, ISO extended nonowned coverage for named individuals PP 03 06 may be attached to the personal auto policy. All family members that should be covered must be listed. The endorsement deletes exclusions B.2. and B.3., so that family members other than "you" driving a company car are covered. (The endorsement also responds to the insured's personal use of a company car.) Or perhaps there is no personal car in the household, but auto coverage is an umbrella requirement. A named nonowner policy should be considered. If using the ISO forms, it is endorsement PP 03 22. Exclusions B.2. and B.3 are amended so that the references to "regularly furnished" are deleted, so personal use of a company vehicle is covered.

Caution! If using the named nonowner form, then each family member who should be covered must be named on the endorsement. There is no (repeat, *no*) automatic coverage for a resident spouse or other family members.

Family Autos Titled to a Business

A common way for a business owner to shift risk away from personal assets is to title the family vehicles in the name of the business. Therefore, in regards to a personal umbrella, there is no underlying personal auto policy in place unless one of two things happens. First, a named nonowner policy may be purchased, or second, the business auto policy may be endorsed to provide coverage. Remember, the personal umbrella provides broad coverage that is designed to cover the insured's use of any covered vehicle. A business auto policy, unless so written or endorsed, will not automatically cover an insured's use of a borrowed or rented car. (Of course, the commercial auto symbol 1 is "any auto," and that includes owned and nonowned vehicles.)

A business auto policy may be endorsed by adding drive other car coverage—broadened coverage for named individuals CA 99 10 or individual named insured CA 99 17. If the CA 99 10 is used, care must be taken that family members other than the spouse (who is automatically covered) are named; otherwise they will not be considered insureds. If the CA 99 17 is added, then family members of the named insured are considered insureds for any covered auto of the private passenger type and owned by the named insured. They are also insureds for the use of nonowned autos (certain restrictions apply; see the endorsement. See also *Business Auto Coverage Guide,* National Underwriter Co., 1998 for more information.) Remember that generally the personal umbrella responds to losses that are covered by underlying insurance. Often, if there is a corporately-titled vehicle involved, the personal umbrella underwriter will want to make sure that such vehicles are properly insured.

No Vehicle? What Then?

We then come to the situation in which the insured has no company car and does not own a vehicle, but may drive a borrowed or rental vehicle. In this case, endorsement PP 03 22 named nonowner coverage is attached to the PAP. The individual for whom the coverage is written is to be listed in the schedule or declarations. Named nonowner coverage may be extended to family members (as defined in the PAP) including the named individual's spouse. Coverage for vehicles furnished or available for regular use may be purchased; if this is indicated on the schedule then the exclusions for vehicles furnished or available for regular use in part A – Liability and part B – Medical Payments do not apply. Use of this endorsement enables someone who does not own a car to meet the requirements for an umbrella policy.

Sometimes an umbrella insurer will not write an umbrella over an auto exposure it does not insure. In other cases, the umbrella insurer will consider an umbrella if it writes the commercial auto account. Each case is different. If a client has a company car, review underlying policies carefully and check with the personal umbrella underwriter to see how this exposure should be handled.

Exclusions for Motor Vehicles

Business Use

Normal business usage of insureds' vehicles is covered. The salesman making calls, the carpenter taking his pickup to a job site, etc., all may be covered under a personal auto policy, and, therefore, on a personal umbrella. Remember that personal automobile insurance has a rate specifically for business use. The personal umbrella forms do not preclude coverage in this situation.

The ISO form has an exception for use of an auto in the auto business. It is essentially the same as that found in the PAP (exclusion 6.). There is liability coverage for:

(4) The use of an "auto" you own, or a temporary substitute for such "auto", by you, a "family member" or a partner, agent or employee of you or a "family member" while employed or otherwise engaged in the "business" of:

(a) Selling;

(b) Repairing;

(c) Servicing;

(d) Storing; or

(e) Parking;

vehicles designed for use mainly on public highways;

(5) The use of an "auto" for "business" purposes, other than an auto business, by an "insured".

Neither the AAIS nor the MSO forms have a similar statement of coverage; relying, perhaps, on the statement that there is no coverage unless there is underlying coverage, or that the underlying coverage limits have been exhausted.

Uber and Others

There is growing popularity for Uber, Lyft, and other commercial enterprises whereby a driver uses his or her personal vehicle to make some extra money. There are some situations where a driver may leave his or her keys available, for a charge, for anyone needing to run errands etc. This is certainly not the venue to discuss their pros and cons, but the fact is they do exist. The PAP clearly states that there is no liability coverage: "For that insured's liability arising out of the ownership or operation of a vehicle while it is being used as a public or livery conveyance. This exclusion (A.5) does not apply to a share-the-expense car pool." The form is stating that if a vehicle is held out to the public as a taxi then there is no coverage. And, of course, with no underlying coverage in place there will be no umbrella coverage. (Remember, though, that the teenager occasionally using his or her vehicle to deliver pizza will be covered, since the vehicle is not being held out to the public for use.)

The ISO umbrella form declines to cover this exposure, with two exclusions stating that the coverages do not apply to:

4. "Bodily injury" or "property damage" arising out of the ownership or operation of an "auto" while it is being used as a public or livery conveyance. This exclusion (A.4.) does not apply to:

    a. A share-the-expense car pool; or

    b. The ownership or operation of an "auto" while it is being used for volunteer or charitable purposes;

5. "Bodily injury" or "property damage" arising out of the ownership, maintenance or use of an "auto" while:

    a. Enrolled in a personal vehicle sharing program under the terms of a written agreement; and

    b. Being used in connection with such personal vehicle sharing program by anyone other than you or any "family member."

The AAIS exclusion is less elaborate, but also says that the personal umbrella coverage does not apply in certain circumstances, and then gives this exception (and an exclusion):

> f. to the use of a "motorized vehicle", but only to the extent that such use is covered by "underlying insurance" at the time of the "occurrence" or offense or would have been covered but for the exhaustion of its "limits".

However, regardless of the terms of the "underlying insurance", this Personal Umbrella Liability Coverage does not apply to "bodily injury", "personal injury", or "property damage" arising out of the use of a "motorized vehicle" as a public or livery conveyance, other than a share-the-expense car pool.

The MSO form excludes liability coverage for aircraft, motor vehicles, and watercraft, but then goes on to state that the exclusion does not apply to the extent that coverage for such is provided in underlying primary insurance.

Racing

Both the AAIS and ISO forms preclude coverage for racing an auto. The PAP only specifically excludes coverage for any vehicle *located inside a facility designed for racing* (italics added) for the purpose of competing in or practicing for any prearranged or organized racing or speed contest. But the AAIS and ISO umbrella forms close any potential gap. The AAIS form, in exclusion 18, eliminates coverage for:

> "bodily injury" or "property damage" arising out of the use of a "motorized vehicle" in or in the practice or the preparation for a prearranged or organized racing, speed, pulling or pushing, demolition, or stunt activity or contest.

The ISO form will not provide liability coverage for:

13. The ownership, maintenance or use of:
    a. Any "auto" for the purpose of:
        (1) Participating or competing in; or
        (2) Practicing or preparing for;

        any prearranged or organized:

        (a) Racing or speed contest; or
        (b) Driver skill training or driver skill event.

Again, the MSO form refers to underlying coverage and its lack thereof.

Permissive Use

The ISO form contains another exclusion not found specifically in the MSO. The umbrella will not provide coverage for:

12. A person using an "auto", "recreational motor vehicle" or watercraft without a reasonable belief that that person is entitled to do so. This exclusion (A.12.) does not apply to a "family member" using an "auto", "recreational motor vehicle" or watercraft you own.

In the AAIS form, the exclusion is located in the definition of "insured": "No person is an 'insured' with respect to the use of a 'motorized vehicle'… unless that person has a reasonable expectation that he or she has a right to such use." And, as in the ISO form, this does not apply to a vehicle that the named insured owns or leases.

We discussed the concept of a "permissive user" above.

Entrustment—Negligent Supervision

The AAIS form in several exclusions precludes coverage for entrustment (of a motor vehicle) or negligent supervision. There is no exclusion in the PAP; however, the homeowners forms contain exclusions for negligent entrustment and/or supervision. Obviously, the homeowners forms do not provide coverage for use of an auto—the motorized vehicle referred to in homeowners forms is generally a golf cart, snowmobile, ATV, etc. However, in the past, when auto limits became exhausted (usually following a traumatic auto accident which often involved a young driver), it was not uncommon for a claimant to sue charging the parents had negligently entrusted a vehicle to their child, or, on the other hand, had neglected to supervise the child. Before the exclusions were added, these theories of negligence found some favor with the courts. Now, the gap has been closed with regard to the homeowners policies, and the AAIS umbrella seeks to do the same. The AAIS umbrella does state that there is coverage if there is underlying insurance that would apply.

And Finally…

The MSO, AAIS, and ISO umbrellas have an exclusion to be mindful of, and that is for no fault, UM, or UIM. The MSO form declares that "*We* do not cover *bodily injury, property damage,* or *personal injury* for which benefits are required by law to be provided or made available to an *insured* under any automobile no-fault, uninsured motorist, or underinsured motorist law or similar law." The AAIS form states: "Regardless of the terms of the 'underlying insurance', this Personal Umbrella Liability Coverage does not provide automobile no fault or any similar coverage, uninsured motorists coverage or underinsured motorists coverage or any similar coverage, or automobile medical expense, automobile medical payments, or any similar coverage." Finally, the ISO form says:

C. We do not provide:

1. Automobile no-fault or any similar coverage under this Policy; or
2. Uninsured Motorists Coverage, Underinsured Motorists Coverage, or any similar coverage unless this Policy is endorsed to provide such coverage.

Thus, the ISO form recognizes the possibility that UM might be required to be offered, or, if not required, at least be offered.

We have not mentioned all exclusions relevant to a motor vehicle. We will look at other exclusions in the next chapter, since many of the motor vehicles covered by an umbrella are recreational vehicles. One final exclusion to mention, though, and that is found only in the MSO umbrella. Although the exclusion for bodily injury, property damage, or personal injury arising out of maintenance, use, operation, etc. of a motor vehicle does not apply to the extent there is underlying insurance, the form states:

> But *we* do not cover *bodily injury*, *property damage*, or *personal injury* arising out of newly acquired... *motor vehicles* ... unless we are notified within 30 days of such acquisition.

Keep in mind that MSO does not have an auto form, and so many of the umbrella insureds might well have coverage on the ISO PAP. When an insured refers to his or her auto policy, he or she might see that a "newly acquired auto" is required to be reported to the insurer depending upon the coverage desired. However, if the "newly acquired auto" simply replaces a vehicle already insured, coverage is provided without the insured requesting it. (Of course, if the newly acquired auto is a 2016 Lexus replacing a 2000 Toyota Camry, then the insured will probably take the initiative and report the change.) The MSO umbrella does not distinguish between a "newly acquired auto" (nonetheless define the term) and thus anyone insured on a PAP should be made aware that the umbrella insurer requires any such vehicle be reported.

Foreign Travel

Personal umbrella policies respond to covered occurrences anywhere in the world. This includes auto accidents. Indeed, a reason to purchase an umbrella policy has traditionally been its providing primary coverage for accidents occurring outside the United States, its territories and possessions, Canada, or Puerto Rico. Some umbrella insurers, however, are eliminating this coverage, and require the insured to carry underlying auto insurance limits which may be at least as high as those normally required for umbrella coverage. Failure to do so results in the umbrella's responding to a covered loss as if the required coverage had been in place. In other words, the umbrella will not drop down to fill in the coverage gap.

If any of your clients rent vehicles abroad, then check the umbrella policy, or with the insurer, in advance to find what is required.

Chapter 5

Recreational Motor Vehicles and Other Fun Stuff

Introduction

The three umbrella forms we are reviewing—ISO, AAIS, and MSO, all provide limited coverage for liability arising out of the use of recreational motor vehicles. This is, of course, also true with regard to the respective homeowners forms. As we have frequently noted in the previous chapters, coverage often depends upon there being underlying coverage. Now, most insureds understand that they have liability coverage for their private passenger autos provided by their auto policy; likewise, they have personal liability provided by their homeowners policy (many persons view homeowners coverage as applying only to accidents occurring on the residence premises, so a certain amount of agent-provided education is often in order). But with regard to liability arising out of the use of, say, a snowmobile or a golf cart, or a 75 HP outboard on pontoon boat, unfortunately the response is "Huh? Isn't this covered?"

Therefore, anyone purchasing an umbrella should be carefully questioned about their "toys." After-the-fact is simply too late. By way of example—a neighbor parks his ski-boat in his garage. Given the fact that during the summer he takes it out on the nearby river, and given its cost, he probably has insurance. But what he probably hasn't divulged to his insurance agent is that during the warm weather he lets his kids drive his golf cart up and down the public street in front of his house.

We will begin this chapter looking at motorized recreations vehicles, including who is an insured for their usage, and then go on to look at the definitions of these vehicles. We will review coverage available on the homeowners forms, including ways to provide additional coverage by endorsement. We will look at ISO's motorcycle form. We'll discuss the pertinent exclusions for recreational motor vehicle usage. We will then move on to a discussion of watercraft liability, and conclude with a brief paragraph on aircraft.

Although we review the coverage under the homeowners forms, this is not intended to be a complete discussion. For more information, see the *Homeowners Coverage Guide*, Fifth Edition.

Motorized Recreational Vehicles

Who Is an Insured

We have already discussed "who is an insured" with regard to use of a private passenger auto (or motorized vehicle). The same definitions apply with regard to a motorized recreational vehicle, with a few differences to be aware of. In the MSO, ISO, and AAIS homeowners policies, there is coverage for persons in the employment of the insured with regard to a motorized vehicle to which the policy applies (as a golf cart), and for other persons using such a vehicle (a snowmobile, perhaps) on an insured location. These persons are insured only if using the vehicle with the insured's consent. So, for example, if Jeeves the Butler is asked to take Madame's painting supplies to her garden shed/woman cave, and uses the ATV to cross the residence premises, he is covered as an insured. (In the MSO form there is no coverage for an employee in the course of a business as defined.) However, there is no direct mention of this coverage applying in the umbrella policies; rather, coverage is given indirectly. The ISO form refers to the exception for the "recreational motor vehicle liability" exclusion as not applicable to a vehicle owned by the named insured or a family member to the extent that there is underlying insurance coverage; the AAIS form also says the exclusion for use of a motorized vehicle does not apply to the extent such use is covered by underlying insurance. The MSO form refers to coverage being provided in underlying insurance.

Definitions of a Recreational Motor Vehicle

Virtually all umbrellas contain some definition of a recreational motor vehicle. In the case of ISO, MSO, and AAIS, they range from comprehensive (ISO) to almost nonexistent. The thing to keep in mind, however, is that one should always check the vehicle to be covered, and then check the policy, *then* recheck both the policy and the vehicle for coverage. There are so many motorized vehicles—from a Segway to a Harley-Davidson—that often the safest practice is to assume liability coverage will need to be endorsed to the homeowners or added through a separate policy. Let's start with the AAIS umbrella definition:

"Motorized vehicle" means:

a. a self-propelled land or amphibious vehicle regardless of method of surface contact...

b. a trailer or semitrailer that:

    1) is attached to or being carried on or towed by; or

2) becomes detached while being carried on or towed by;

a vehicle described in a. above.

The ISO definition is more specific as to a recreational motor vehicle:

"Recreational motor vehicle: means:

1. All-terrain vehicle;
2. Dune buggy;
3. Golf car;
4. Snowmobile; or
5. Any other motorized land vehicle which is designed for recreational use off public roads.

Lest it appear that the ISO definition has overlooked a trailer, remember that the ISO umbrella form has a definition for "auto" that encompasses trailers, motor homes, and other such items. The definition for an "auto" also includes a moped or a motorcycle. (Refer to Chapter 4.)

Finally, the MSO form simply states that a *motor vehicle* is "any self-propelled land vehicle, semi-trailer or trailer including any equipment or machinery attached to such."

Because the umbrella forms all refer to coverage based upon underlying coverage, we should also turn to the respective homeowners forms. In the AAIS homeowners form, the definition for a motorized vehicle is identical to that in the umbrella form. In the ISO homeowners form, there is no separate definition for a recreational motor vehicle; rather, the form says a motor vehicle means:

a. a self-propelled land or amphibious vehicle; or

b. any trailer or semi-trailer which is being carried on, towed by or hitched for towing by a vehicle described in a. above.

It is only in the ISO homeowners exclusions that we see that some motor vehicles are "designed for recreational use off public roads" or golf carts.

In the MSO homeowners form, there is no definition at all. Rather, it is only in the "Incidental Motorized Land Vehicle and Trailer Coverage Section" that we learn what the insurer considers to be recreational vehicles, and these are golf carts, vehicles designed for recreational use off public roads, and boat, camp, home or utility trailers if not attached to, carried on, or towed by a motor vehicle other than a golf cart, recreational vehicle designed for use off public roads, etc.

Coverage under the Homeowners Forms

Now let's take a look at the coverage for these vehicles on the unendorsed homeowners forms. We'll use the ISO definition, since the AAIS and the MSO are similar. Differences, though, will be noted. The ISO homeowners form gives coverage by means of exceptions to the exclusion for "motor vehicle liability," while the AAIS form provides coverage as incidental liability coverage for motorized vehicles. Likewise, the MSO form refers to incidental motorized land vehicle and trailer coverage. Remember that once a trailer, such as a camper, is detached from the motor vehicle towing it, it is no longer considered a motor or motorized vehicle. Note—that means it *is* detached, not becomes detached. If a camper becomes detached from the vehicle towing it, liability follows the vehicle doing the towing. But once the camper is parked and unattached, liability coverage is found in the homeowners policy.

The ISO homeowners form declares there is coverage for a motor vehicle:

d. Designed for recreational use off public roads and:

  (1) Not owned by an "insured"; or

  (2) Owned by an "insured" provided the "occurrence" takes place:

    (a) On an "insured location" as defined in Definition B.6.a., b., d., e. or h; [Note: premises used in connection with premises a. or b., land on which a dwelling is being built, and cemetery plots do not qualify] or

    b) Off an "insured location" and the "motor vehicle" is:

      (i) Designed as a toy vehicle for use by children under seven years of age;

      (ii) Powered by one or more batteries; and

      (iii) Not built or modified after manufacture to exceed a speed of five miles per hour on level ground; [Note: the AAIS provision states the vehicle cannot exceed a speed of 15 miles per hour, and cannot be a motorized bicycle, moped, or golf cart—coverage for a golf cart is included in another AAIS provision.]

e. A motorized golf cart that is owned by an "insured", designed to carry up to four persons, not built or modified after manufacture to exceed a speed of 25 miles per hour on level ground and, at the time of the "occurrence", is within the legal boundaries of:

(1) A golfing facility and is parked or stored there, or being used by an "insured" to:

(a) Play the game of golf or for other recreational or leisure activity allowed by the facility;

(b) Travel to or from an area where "motor vehicles" or golf carts are parked or stored; or

(c) Cross public roads at designated points to access other parts of the golfing facility; or

(2) A private residential community, including its public roads upon which a motorized golf cart can legally travel, which is subject to the authority of a property owners association and contains an "insured's" residence.

The MSO coverage is similar—coverage exists for the use of a golf cart while playing golf, including travel from a parking area and crossing a road to access the golf facility. There is also coverage for an insured's use of a nonowned recreational motor vehicle (one designed for use off public roads) or for the use of a recreational motor vehicle on the insured premises. The AAIS liability coverage wording is similar to that of the ISO form.

Having looked at the coverages for recreational motor vehicles, we review the exclusions. Remember, all the umbrella forms state that there is no coverage for certain occurrences if there is no underlying insurance. The MSO form is different in that there are no explicit exclusions for recreational motor vehicles; rather, the form states in the incidental liability section what *is* covered, not what *isn't* covered. The ISO homeowners form, in the exclusions for "motor vehicle liability," reminds the insured that there is no coverage if, at the time and place of an "occurrence": the motor vehicle is registered for use on public roads or property; is not so registered but such registration is required for it to be used at the place of the "occurrence"; is being operated in or practicing for an organized race or contest; used to carry persons or cargo for a charge; or used for any "business" purpose, except for a golf cart while on a golf facility. The AAIS form is similar.

Having mentioned snowmobiles—many northern states such as Michigan and Minnesota require snowmobile registration. So, simply thinking the exclusion will not apply could leave an insured lacking should an accident occur. In this event, it might be more prudent to provide coverage other than that found in the unendorsed homeowners form.

How, then, can coverage be put in place for an insured? ISO has endorsements that can be used with the homeowners form, such as HO 24 13 05 11 incidental low power recreational motor vehicle liability coverage endorsement. There is liability coverage for a vehicle designed for recreation use off public roads, and not owned by an insured, or owned by an insured and on an insured location. There is coverage if the vehicle is off an insured location, provided that the vehicle was not built or modified to exceed fifteen miles per hour, and is not a motorized bicycle, motorized scooter, moped, or golf cart. This endorsement could be used if the unendorsed homeowners limitation of five miles per hour is not adequate to insure a child's replica Humvee. Endorsement HO 24 64 10 00 owned snowmobile provides liability coverage for an occurrence taking place off an insured location (as defined).

ISO has two other ways to write coverage for motorized recreational vehicles. The first is the PAP, which may be endorsed with PP 03 23 01 05 miscellaneous type vehicle endorsement to cover a motor home, motorcycle or similar type vehicle, all-terrain vehicle, dune buggy, or golf cart. The personal motorcycle policy MT 00 01 12 13 may be endorsed with MT 03 08 12 13 recreational vehicle endorsement, which then gives coverage for ATVs, dirt bikes, dune buggies, golf carts, mopeds, motorscooters, motorbikes, or go-karts. To cover a snowmobile, endorsement MT 03 13 may be attached to the motorcycle policy.

Now, neither MSO nor AAIS have motorcycle forms (or a personal auto policy). The AAIS homeowners form can be endorsed with HO 3832 golf cart liability, HO 3864 snowmobile liability—off premises, HO 3828 motorized vehicle liability coverage—low power vehicles (no motor bikes, mopeds, or golf carts, and restricted to vehicles under fifteen miles per hour). Endorsement HO 1539 motorized vehicles may be attached where allowed. The MSO program has no similar endorsements.

Before leaving the topic of coverage for motorized recreational motor vehicles, we look at liability coverage for a recreational motor vehicle in an insured's care, custody, or control.

Homeowners forms do not usually provide liability coverage for property in the care, custody, or control of an insured, except for property damage to property rented to, occupied or used by or in the care of an insured caused by fire, smoke or explosion (often referred to as fire legal coverage). That is not to say there is no coverage for damage to property of others—the coverage C insuring agreement declares that there is coverage for personal property owned by *or used by* an insured while it is anywhere in the world. So, a borrowed snowmobile that an insured wraps around a tree would be covered as personal property, right?

Well, no. The ISO homeowners HO 00 03 05 11 form, under "property not covered," clearly states "We do not cover… 'motor vehicles,'" which are "self-propelled land or amphibious vehicles." But if we look at the liability coverage for "damage to property of others," we find that up to $1,000 is available for this loss. The form excludes damage arising out of the ownership, maintenance, occupancy, operation, use, loading or unloading of aircraft, hovercraft, watercraft, or "motor vehicles," but then excepts coverage for a motor vehicle that:

(a) is designed for recreational use off public roads;

(b) is not owned by an "insured"; and

(c) at the time of the occurrence, is not required by law, or regulation issued by a governmental agency, to have been registered for it to be used on public roads or property.

The AAIS HO 0003 09 08 homeowners form grants the same amount of coverage. The MSO form MPL 01 11, however, does not provide any coverage for loss "arising out of… maintenance, ownership, or use of aircraft, motorized vehicles, or watercraft."

Motorcycles

We mentioned motorcycles in connection with writing a policy for snowmobiles and other recreational motor vehicles. The ISO PAP may be endorsed with the miscellaneous vehicles endorsement PP 03 23. Alternatively, ISO personal motorcycle policy MT 00 01 12 13 may be used. The motorcycle form MT 00 01 12 13 has several exclusions, such as there is no liability coverage for anyone operating a motorcycle while under the influence of alcohol or a controlled substance. Note that this is unlike the personal auto policy, which does not eliminate coverage for a drunk driver.

Therefore, before assuming an umbrella insurer will provide liability coverage for these vehicles, it might be wise to ask. Also, the umbrella insurer might well request that there be no passenger hazard exclusion. Rates are cheaper with the exclusion, which effectively eliminates coverage for bodily injury to a passenger, but without the exclusion the possibility of a long, drawn-out lawsuit remains. The insurer might also request that there be no lay-up period; in other words, the liability coverage is to be kept in effect year-round.

Exclusions on the Homeowners (and Umbrella) Forms

We will discuss the homeowners and umbrella exclusions together. Remember that if there is no underlying coverage for recreational motor vehicles, there will be no umbrella coverage. We discussed the coverage available both through the unendorsed homeowners policy and by means of endorsement in **Coverage under the Homeowners Forms** above.

First, the ISO homeowners form defines "motor vehicle liability":

> Liability for "bodily injury" or "property damage" arising out of the:
>
> (1) Ownership of such vehicle or craft by an "insured";
>
> (2) Maintenance, occupancy, operation, use, loading or unloading of such vehicle or craft by any person;
>
> (3) Entrustment of such vehicle or craft by an "insured" to any person;
>
> (4) Failure to supervise or negligent supervision of any person involving such vehicle or craft by an "insured"' or
>
> (5) Vicarious liability, whether or not imposed by law, for the actions of a child or minor involving such vehicle or craft.

This wording is repeated in the ISO umbrella form. However, just as the homeowners form gives back coverage through means of exceptions (discussed above), so does the ISO umbrella form: "Recreational Motor Vehicle Liability"… However, this exclusion (A.10) does not apply with respect to any "recreational motor vehicle": owned by you or a "family member" to the extent that "recreational motor vehicle" coverage is provided by "underlying insurance" at the time of the "occurrence"; or that you or a "family member does not own." (The ISO umbrella form also states that there is coverage if the insured is participating in motorcycle skill training in connection with a course designed by the Motorcycle Safety Foundation, or any similar course administered by any state agency, to improve motorcycle rider skills. This exception is also found in the motorcycle policy.)

The AAIS homeowners form, likewise, precludes coverage for "bodily injury" or "property damage" arising out of:

> 1) the ownership or leasing of a "motorized vehicle" or "watercraft" by an "insured";
>
> 2) the operation, maintenance, use, occupancy, loading, or unloading of a "motorized vehicle" or "watercraft" by any person;
>
> 3) the entrustment or loaning of a "motorized vehicle" or "watercraft" by an "insured" to any person; or
>
> 4) an "insured's" negligent supervision, or failure to supervise, any person with respect to a "motorized vehicle" or "watercraft".

Though it appears that the AAIS homeowners form eliminates coverage for negligent entrustment or supervision, this is not the case. Rather, the AAIS form gives incidental coverage for certain watercraft and motorized vehicles, and then states that the exclusion for property damage or bodily injury arising from these does not apply to those craft and vehicles: "However, this exclusion does not apply to 'bodily injury' … if coverage is provided under the Incidental Liability Coverage for Motorized Vehicles or the Incidental Liability Coverage for Watercraft."

The AAIS umbrella form repeats this wording, but adds that "Except as stated in the following paragraphs, this exclusion does not apply to the extent that such 'bodily injury' or 'property damage' is covered by underlying insurance at the time of the 'occurrence' or would have been covered but for the exhaustion of its 'limits'". The AAIS umbrella form also eliminates coverage for bodily injury or property damage arising out of the ownership, etc., of an aircraft or hovercraft, including vicarious liability or negligent supervision or entrustment.

The MSO homeowners form declares that there is no coverage for bodily injury or property damage arising out of:

A. The maintenance, operation, ownership, or use (including loading or unloading) of any aircraft, motor vehicle, or watercraft owned or operated by, or rented or loaned to, any *insured*.

B. The entrustment to others, whether or not under any form of supervision, of any aircraft, motor vehicle, or watercraft.

See supplemental Coverages 7 and 8 for limited coverage.

Then, the MSO umbrella repeats, for the most, the above exclusions, but in the second exclusion adds there is no coverage for statutory vicarious liability of parents for acts of minors using an aircraft, motor vehicle, or watercraft. Of course, if there is underlying primary coverage, the umbrella responds.

Having listed the homeowners forms' exclusions, we note there is an exception in the MSO, AAIS, and ISO homeowners forms for bodily injury (as defined) to a residence employee arising out of and in the course of employment by an insured. The AAIS umbrella form states that the exclusion for bodily injury or property damage arising out of an aircraft or hovercraft does not apply to bodily injury to a domestic employee arising out of and in the course of his or her employment by an insured. Nothing in the ISO or MSO umbrella forms makes reference to this; however, because there is coverage in the underlying homeowners forms coverage should extend to the umbrella forms.

There is one final exclusion to note, and that is the exclusion of coverage for recreational vehicles and watercraft while practicing for or being used in any prearranged or organized race, stunt activity, speed contest, or other competition. This exclusion does not apply to sail boats or to watercraft involved in predicted log cruises. Neither the MSO homeowners nor the umbrella mention this.

In Chapter 4 we mentioned the theory of negligence used to find coverage in the homeowners policies for, say, the action of a minor involved in a motorized vehicle accident. We noted above the exclusions in the homeowners and umbrella forms that preclude coverage for negligent entrustment, negligent supervision, and the like. (But remember that negligent supervision or entrustment arising from the use of a covered motorized vehicle is not excluded.) Three cases illustrate how this works (and why the courts uphold the exclusions for negligent supervision and negligent entrustment).

The first case, and its outcome, illustrates why in all probability the exclusions have been added to the homeowners and umbrella forms. This first case, involving a mini bike, is *Orville Douglass et al. v. Hartford Insurance Company*, 602 F.2d 934 (Colorado, 1979). Ten-year-old Robert was driving the bike with six-year-old Todd Mahoney as a passenger, apparently looping around the family drive and on to the county road. The bike was struck by a truck. Robert was killed and Todd seriously injured. The insurer refused to defend a possible suit (the statute of limitations would not begin to run until Todd reached the age of majority), citing the exclusion of coverage for "ownership, maintenance, operation, use, loading or unloading" of any recreational motor vehicle away from the premises. But the trial court held, and the appellate court affirmed, "Certainly a mini bike driven by a ten-year-old, with a six-year-old passenger, entering a paved county road, at least invokes the possibility of recovery." Therefore, the insurer was obligated to provide a defense for negligent entrustment.

In this next case, the negligent supervision wording had been added. The appellate court in *Austin Mutual Insurance Company v. Brian D. Klande et al.*, 563 N.W.2d 282 (Minnesota, 1997), reviewed an exclusion for bodily injury or property damage resulting directly or indirectly from "the ownership, operation, maintenance, use, occupancy, renting, loaning, entrusting, supervision, loading, or unloading of motorized vehicles" owned by, operated by, or rented or loaned to, an insured and held that the exclusion barred coverage. The Klande's son Mitch, an insured on his parents' homeowners' policy, owned an uninsured motorcycle. One day he gave two young visiting relatives rides on the motorcycle, and afterwards parked the cycle in the garage. One of the youngsters, age nine, wandered into the garage, and attempted to mount the cycle. It fell over on him, and the hot muffler severely burned the child. His mother maintained the Klande's homeowners insurer was obligated to indemnify the insureds for the boy's injuries. A denial of coverage led to an action based on negligent supervision.

The court agreed with the insurer, saying that although it could be possible that two independent acts, one vehicle-related and one not, might combine to cause an injury, in this case the motorcycle was more than just the location of the occurrence. Rather, had the motorcycle not been used for transportation, it would not have become hot. Further, the court held that the motorized vehicle exclusion precluded coverage because the respondents' claim of negligent supervision was not divisible from the ownership and use of the motorcycle itself.

Then, finally, we look at *Iorio v. Simone*, 773 A.2d 722 (N.J. Super. Ct. App. Div. 2001). The insured allowed his son, age twelve, to drive a go-kart with the insured's nine year-old nephew behind. The son drove the kart into the street and hit a tree. The nephew's parents sued, alleging that the negligent supervision occurred on the premises, and therefore the resulting loss should be covered. But the court upheld the exclusion, saying that the trigger should be the accident itself, which took place in an excluded vehicle (it did not meet any of the homeowners criteria for coverage for a recreational motor vehicle), and not the careless conduct of the insured in allowing his son to drive the kart onto the street.

As we stated above, the exclusion for negligent entrustment or negligent supervision does not apply if the cause of the accident is a vehicle for which the homeowners policy provides coverage.

Watercraft

Definitions of Watercraft under Homeowners and Umbrella Policies

The AAIS, MSO, and ISO homeowners and umbrella forms provide limited liability coverage for watercraft. The definitions vary, but in the final analysis the coverage is similar. First, the AAIS homeowners form defines a "watercraft" as "an apparatus or a device primarily designed to be propelled on or in water by engine, motor, or wind, but this does not include:

a. a model watercraft that is not designed or used to carry people or cargo;

b. a "hovercraft";

c. a model hovercraft that is not designed or used to carry people or cargo;

d. a "motorized vehicle";

e. an "aircraft"; or

f. a model aircraft that is not designed or used to carry people or cargo.

The AAIS homeowners form clarifies that this definition is with regard to the liability coverages provided in the policy. The definition in the umbrella form is the same; however, the wording that the definition applies to the liability coverages is omitted—obviously, since the umbrella is a liability policy.

The MSO homeowners form does not define a watercraft. Likewise, there is no definition in the umbrella form. As we will see, it is not until we read the exclusions pertinent to a watercraft that it becomes clear that watercraft powered by means other than an engine or sail are not "watercraft" for liability purposes.

In the ISO homeowners form, a watercraft means: "a craft principally designed to be propelled on or in water by wind, engine power or electric motor." This same definition appears in the ISO umbrella form.

Coverage for Watercraft under Homeowners Policies

The AAIS, MSO, and ISO homeowners forms all provide limited liability coverage for watercraft. The AAIS form covers bodily injury or property damage that arises out of a "watercraft" that:

1) is in storage;

2) is a sailing vessel, with or without auxiliary power, that is:

   a) less than 26 feet in overall length; or

   b) 26 feet or more in overall length and not owned by or rented to an "insured"; or

3) is not a sailing vessel and is powered by:

   a) an inboard or inboard-outdrive engine or motor, including an engine or motor that powers a water jet pump, or:

      (1) 50 horsepower or less if not owned by an "insured"; or

      (2) more than 50 horsepower if not owned by or rented to an "insured"; or

b) one or more outboard engines or motors with:

(1) 25 total horsepower or less;

(2) more than 25 horsepower if the outboard engine or motor is not owned by an "insured";

(3) more than 25 horsepower if the outboard engine or motor is owned by an "insured" who acquired it during the policy period; or

(4) more than 25 horsepower if the outboard engine or motor is owned by an "insured" who acquired it before the policy period, but only if:

(a) it is listed on the "declarations as insured for personal liability; or

(b) a written request for liability coverage is received by "us" within 45 days after it is acquired.

The ISO homeowners form grants coverage for the same sorts of watercraft as the AAIS form. Both AAIS and ISO forms declare that there is no coverage if the watercraft is rented to others, used to carry persons or cargo for a charge, used for any "business" purpose, or used in or in the practice or the preparation for a prearranged or organized racing speed, pulling or pushing, demolition, or stunt activity or contest. The exclusion does not apply, however, to sailboats or a watercraft being used in a predicted log cruise. (Predicted log cruises are those in which the operator predicts exactly how much time he or she will take to complete a certain course, touching certain spots. Speed is not a factor.)

The MSO homeowners form's restrictions on watercraft are similar to those of ISO and AAIS, but do have some differences. For one, notice that the coverage does not extend to a stored watercraft, but only to watercraft while ashore at an insured premises. The MSO form states that:

Coverage E is extended to include *bodily injury* and *property damage* arising out of the following:

A. Sailing vessels, with or without auxiliary power, that are less than 26 feet in length.

B. Watercraft designed to be, and operated as, manually propelled.

C. Watercraft while ashore at an *insured* premises.

D. Watercraft rented to an *insured* with inboard or inboard out drive motor power of less than 50 total rated horsepower.

E. Watercraft not owned by or rented to any *insured* if the occurrence arises out of the direct act of any *insured*.

F. Watercraft powered by one or more outboard motors, as follows:

1. Outboard motors not wholly or partially owned by or leased to any *insured.*

2. Outboard motors owned by or leased to an *insured* that are less than 26 total rated horsepower for all motors combined.

3. Outboard motors owned by or leased to an *insured* that are more than 25 total rated horsepower. But, these must be either acquired during the current policy term; or acquired prior to the current policy term and insured under this policy within 60 days after acquisition.

Note that outboard motors owned by or leased to an insured must be less than twenty-six rated horsepower total for all motors combined, rather than the twenty-five in both ISO and AAIS. Exclusions such as those in AAIS and ISO are found in MSO Section II Liability Not Insured, and are similar.

There are three endorsements that may be attached to homeowners policies to provide liability coverage (yes, correct, liability coverage only—no physical damage coverage). For ISO, endorsement HO 24 75 10 00 allows a watercraft with one or more outboard engines or motors of more than twenty-five total horsepower, or other watercraft with inboard or inboard-outdrive engines or motors, or sailing vessels of twenty-six feet or more overall length, to be scheduled. AAIS offers endorsement HO 3801 01 06, which allows watercraft to be scheduled. Finally, the MSO endorsement is MPL 20 01 02, which may be used to schedule watercraft with outboard, inboard-outdrive, or inboard engines. Additionally, sailboats more than twenty-six feet in length may be scheduled. We should also note that this form has a "customary navigation period" of April 1 to November 1; any differences must be noted on the form.

Boatowners Coverage

ISO and AAIS offer boatowners policies. The ISO form is WT 00 01 01 10 watercraft policy. This form may be used to insure "personal watercraft" such as Jet Skis when endorsement WT 05 01 01 10 is attached; remember, coverage for these is greatly limited in the homeowners form. Check the ISO manual for acceptability, since watercraft with a captain (other than nominally, as the owner—"Cap'n Mark" for example) or crew (except "First Mate Christine") are not eligible.

The AAIS form is BT 0100 05 08. It is intended for boats not over thirty feet in length. It also may be used to cover personal watercraft such as Jet Skis, wave runners, and the like. For boats (yachts) over twenty-six feet in length and valued at over $50,000, form YT 0100 09 10 may be used. This latter form may also be used when a boat is titled to a corporation for tax purposes, so prior to using the form be sure to check with the umbrella underwriter for acceptability. As with thc ISO policy, check the AAIS manual for eligibility. Both the ISO and AAIS forms allow for coverage when the boats are being used for business entertainment purposes. There are no equivalent MSO forms.

Umbrella Watercraft Coverage

This section should more appropriately be entitled "umbrella watercraft exclusions." As we have noted regularly so far, often with regard to motor vehicles, recreational motor vehicles, or watercraft, there is no coverage unless underlying coverage is already in place. As we have seen, the homeowners policies provide limited liability coverage for watercraft. So, if the insured possesses a watercraft with more engine power than the homeowners form covers, or if there is a type of watercraft that is problematic (such as a Jet Ski), then certainly a watercraft policy or special endorsement (where allowed) to the homeowners should be considered. Remember, the umbrella will not drop down to provide coverage where underlying insurance does not exist, either because of, say, a homeowners exclusion, or because the craft in question is insured on a policy that has more coverage restrictions that normally expected. For example, the ISO boatowners form does not exclude coverage for bodily injury or medical payments to a water-skier pulled by the insured's boat, but it is possible that another boatowners form might.

First, we look at the AAIS umbrella exclusions relating to watercraft.

This Personal Umbrella Liability Coverage does not apply to...

16. "bodily injury" or "property damage" arising out of:

    a. the ownership of a "watercraft" by an "insured" or the leasing or renting of a "watercraft" by an "insured" from another;

    b. the operation, maintenance, use, occupancy, loading or unloading of a "watercraft" by any person:

    c. the entrustment or loaning of a "watercraft" by an "insured" to any person; or

    d. an "insured's" negligent supervision of or failure to supervise any person with respect to a "watercraft".

Except as stated in the following paragraphs, this exclusion does not apply to the extent that such "bodily injury" or "property damage" is covered by "underlying insurance" at the time of the "occurrence" or would have been covered but for the exhaustion of its "limits".

Regardless of the terms of the "underlying insurance", this Personal Umbrella Liability Coverage does not apply to "bodily injury" or "property damage" arising out of the use of "watercraft" in or in the practice or the preparation for any prearranged or organized racing, speed, or stunt activities or contests. This does not apply to "watercraft" used in predicted log cruises or to sailing vessels.

Regardless of the terms of the "underlying insurance", this Personal Umbrella Liability Coverage does not provide uninsured boaters coverage or underinsured boaters medical expense, boaters medical payments, or any similar coverage.

17. "bodily injury" or "property damage" for which an "insured" is vicariously liable if the "bodily injury" or "property damage" arises out of the actions of a child or minor with respect to:

    a. a "motorized vehicle"; or

    b. "watercraft".

    This applies whether or not such liability is imposed by law.

    However, this exclusion does not apply to the extent that such liability is covered by "underlying insurance" at the time of the "occurrence" or would have been covered but for the exhaustion of its "limits".

Let's pause for a moment to see how these exclusions—16.a. in particular—work with coverage in the homeowners. Exclusion 16.a. says there is no liability coverage for a rented watercraft. However, the AAIS homeowners incidental liability coverage for watercraft says the insurer will pay for "bodily injury" or "property damage" arising out of a watercraft that "is not a sailing vessel" and is powered by "an inboard or inboard-outdrive engine or motor, including an engine or motor that powers a water jet pump, of (1) 50 horsepower or less if not owned by an "insured." Now, "not owned by an insured" can mean the watercraft is either borrowed by, or rented to, the insured. Therefore, such a watercraft is covered under the homeowners and, by extension, the umbrella. But if the watercraft had an inboard engine of 150 horsepower, it would only be covered by the homeowners policy if it were borrowed. The homeowners form says "more than 50 horsepower if not owned by or rented to an "insured." In both cases the umbrella would provide coverage.

The MSO umbrella form simply states:

1. *Aircraft*; *Motor Vehicles*; Watercraft Exclusion

   A. We do not cover bodily injury, property damage or personal injury arising out of:

      1. The maintenance, operation, ownership, or use (including loading or unloading) of any *aircraft*, *motor vehicle*, or watercraft owned or operated by, or rented or loaned to, any *insured*.

      2. The entrustment to others (whether or not under any form of supervision) of any *aircraft, motor vehicle*, or watercraft; statutory vicarious liability of parents for acts of minors using an *aircraft, motor vehicle*, or watercraft.

   B. This exclusion (Paragraph A) does not apply to the extent that coverage for such is provided in *underlying primary insurance*.

      But we do not cover bodily injury, property damage or personal injury arising out of newly acquired *aircraft, motor vehicles* or watercraft unless we are notified within 30 days of such acquisition.

Remember that MSO has only one form with which to schedule watercraft for liability purposes, MPL 20 01 02. There is no separate boatowners policy. The homeowners exclusions apply, so that form must first be consulted prior to the umbrella's being reviewed.

Finally, we look at the ISO umbrella form. The policy precludes coverage for "bodily injury" or "property damage" arising out of "watercraft liability." The form continues, "However, this exclusion (A.9.) does not apply to the extent that watercraft coverage is provided by "underlying insurance" at the time of the "occurrence." The definition of "watercraft liability" is the same as that for "recreational motor vehicle liability," which we discussed above, except that in this instance "watercraft" must be substituted for "recreational motor vehicle liability."

Let's look at another example as to how the exclusions mesh with the coverage in the underlying policy. In this instance, suppose the insured's son, age nineteen, lives at home. As young men are wont to do, he looks longingly at his friend's Jet Ski, and finally gets up enough nerve to borrow it. The Jet Ski, a Kawasaki Ultra 310 LX, has a MSRP of $17,999, with a 1498 cc engine. Now, this is a borrowed watercraft powered by a water jet pump. But wait, what about the 1498 cc engine? A handy website gives the information that about 32.5 cc is equal to one horsepower. So our borrowed Jet Ski is around 46 HP. That puts the Jet Ski, since it is borrowed and not owned by an insured, within coverage under the homeowners. Therefore, it's covered under the umbrella for liability. So, if the young man accidentally loses control and hits a water skier, there is coverage for bodily injury. Remember, though, if the young man damages the Jet Ski there is no liability coverage for the damage; rather, since the Jet Ski is personal property coverage will fall under the father's homeowners coverage C.

Let's up the ante. The young man convinces his father that he will be a responsible Jet Ski owner, and so doting father offers to buy a Kawasaki STX 15 F, MSRP $10,000, horsepower 160; 62 MPH speed. Same scenario as above, except this time the young man is riding his own (well, his father's) Jet Ski when he injures a water skier. No coverage. The watercraft is owned and more than fifty HP. No coverage under the umbrella, either. Unless, of course, the father has called his insurance agent, and after reading the policy to the insured, she told him that he should purchase a boatowners policy. And since his insurance form is already an ISO form, she's reviewed the ISO boatowners form WT 00 01 01 10, and will add endorsement WT 05 01 01 10. The insured told his agent to please go ahead, and mentioned he's found another really neat toy—a Renegade Hovercraft for only $27,900! (Hopefully at this point the agent wakes to find this last was a dream.)

One final precaution: check all forms carefully to find out when a newly acquired watercraft (or recreational vehicle, for that matter) must be reported to the insurer.

Airplanes

None of the personal umbrella forms we've reviewed provide liability coverage for aircraft, except for model aircraft not designed for carrying persons or cargo. Having said this, both the ISO and AAIS homeowners forms state that the aircraft liability exclusions do not apply to "bodily injury" to a "residence employee" (ISO) or "domestic employee" arising out of and in the course of employment by an insured. However, the ISO umbrella form does not mention this exception, while the AAIS umbrella form states that the exclusions for "bodily injury" or "property damage" arising out of aircraft or hovercraft (ownership, loading, entrustment, etc.) do not apply to "bodily injury" to a "domestic employee" in the course of his or her employment by an insured. Neither the MSO homeowners form nor the umbrella form address this. As of this writing the issue of recreational drones is still being discussed. Currently they may be considered model aircraft, but it may not stay that way in the future.

Chapter 6

Exclusions: Part I

Introduction

Just as there is no "standard" umbrella form, so there is no consistency with regard to exclusions. Even the three forms we are discussing—MSO, AAIS, and ISO—differ as to exclusions. And, as we have seen in the previous chapters, methods for providing acceptable underlying coverage vary as well. Even where one might think to find an exclusion—such as for bodily injury or property damage arising out of business activities—some forms excluded coverage altogether, but others excluded coverage unless underlying coverage was scheduled on the declarations. The safest thing, when confronted with a questionable situation, is certainly to ask questions first, and, if you are an agent, to make sure that your client is aware of any potential gaps.

This chapter examines exclusions that occur in the three forms: business (care, custody, and control); intentional acts; and the intrafamily exclusion. In Chapter 7 we'll discuss personal injury, pollution, war, workers comp, and exclusions that do not appear in all of the forms.

"Business" Exclusions

Although an exclusion of coverage for activities arising out of a business is common to all the umbrellas surveyed, they are not alike in the treatment of this exclusion, except in one respect. That is, the use of a private passenger auto used for business purposes other than taxi or livery service is covered. So, for example, an insured driving his or her own auto on sales calls is covered. Likewise, an insured driving a company-furnished car to make sales calls is covered, provided the applicable insurance is in place (see Chapter 4).

We gave the homeowners forms' business definitions in Chapter 2, "Definitions". Remember, if there is no coverage under an underlying policy, often, but not always, there will be no coverage under the umbrella—unless, of course, the underlying policy may be endorsed to provide the required insurance.

The MSO homeowners form excludes coverage for bodily injury or property damage arising out of business (as defined) activities of any insured. However, the MSO form holds that some activities are not "business" in nature, such as "activities, other than child care, that may relate to business of the insured but are not done for business and are otherwise covered by this policy." For example, an insured might accidentally bump against someone and knock them down while out for dinner with a business associate after work; this is related to business but is not a business activity in and of itself. Then, the policy also covers cashier, clerical or sales activities other than those involving demonstration, installation, or servicing, unless the insured owns or operates the business. (Those with a long history in insurance will recognize the latter as having been a part of earlier homeowners forms.) Part-time or seasonal activities of a student less than twenty-one years of age who is self-employed with no other employee are also covered. Note that, unlike the ISO and AAIS forms, there is no dollar amount per year limitation. The MSO homeowners policy also considers that the following activities, for liability purposes, are not "business" in nature:

D. Rental of the insured premises customarily occupied by you:

1. On an occasional basis for use solely as a residence.
2. In part, for use solely as a residence with no more than 2 lodgers per family unit.
3. In part, for use as an office, private garage, school, or studio.

In the MSO program, coverage for certain business activities may be endorsed to the homeowners policy. Home-based business coverage endorsement MPL 58 and MPL 52 incidental business coverage-sections I and II may be used.

The MSO umbrella form excludes business activities:

> We do not cover *bodily injury*, *property damage*, or *personal injury* arising out of any *business* activities.

The form goes on, though, to state:

> But this exclusion does not apply to the extent that coverage for such activities is provided in *underlying primary insurance*.

Therefore, actions such as renting a room to a lodger, renting office space, etc., have liability coverage under the homeowners policy and also under the umbrella.

Like the MSO form, the AAIS homeowners form has incidental business coverage for business (as defined; the dollar limit is $2,500 per year) activities of an insured under the age of 21, when self-employed with no other employees. The AAIS homeowners policy may be endorsed with HO 3542 office, professional, private school, or studio occupancy to cover this type of exposure on the insured premises. The home-based business endorsement is ML-450.

However, the AAIS umbrella form's exclusion for business, unlike that of MSO, appears absolute (although coverage may be added by endorsement):

This Personal Umbrella Liability Coverage does not apply to:

1. "bodily injury", "personal injury", or "property damage" arising out of or in any way related to a "business":

    a. conducted from any part of a premises, or vacant land, owned by or leased or rented to an "insured"' or

    b. undertaken by an "insured", regardless of location;

    whether or not the "business" is owned or operated by an "insured" or employs an "insured" and whether or not the "bodily injury", "personal injury", or "property damage" is covered by "underlying insurance" at the time of the "occurrence" or offense.

Excepted from this exclusion are "business" activities of an "insured" under age twenty-one, if self-employed with no employees, civic or public activities, occasional rental of premises for use as a residence, rental to no more than two roomers or lodgers, leasing or rental of part of the insured premises for use as a school, studio, office, or private garage, and rental of an insured premises other than that occupied by the named insured—such as a rental property that is covered by underlying insurance.

Though there is no reference to coverage for "business" activities if there is underlying coverage, coverage may be added through endorsement (and underwriter approval). AAIS has endorsements PU 1636 01 14 personal umbrella liability coverage—business activities, and PU 06 30 10 11 specified business activities. Consult the manual for more information.

There is coverage, though, for an insured's service as an officer or member of a board of directors for a not for profit organization, so long as the insured is not in any way employed or compensated by the organization, other than reimbursement of expenses.

The ISO umbrella form eliminates coverage for "bodily injury," "property damage," or "personal injury" arising out of or in connection with a "business:

a. Engaged in by an "insured"' or

b. Conducted from:

(1) Any part of a premises owned by or rented to an "insured"; or

(2) Vacant land owned by or rented to an "insured".

This exclusion applies but is not limited to an act or omission, regardless of its nature or circumstance, involving a service or duty rendered, promised, owed, or implied to be provided because of the nature of the "business".

Like the AAIS umbrella, the ISO form states the exclusion does not apply to the rental of the residence premises on an occasional basis for use as a residence, in part, as an office, school, studio or private garage, for rent of a single-family unit to no more than two roomers or boarders. "Bodily injury", "property damage", or "personal injury" arising out of an act or omission of an "insured" as an officer or member of a board of directors of a corporation or organization and excluded, unless the corporation or organization is not-for-profit and the insured receives no compensation other than reimbursement of expenses.

The ISO form also grants coverage for rental of a one-to-four family dwelling, other than the residence premises, and to a condo, cooperative, or apartment unit other than the residence premises so long as underlying coverage is in place.

As with the AAIS form, the ISO form does not state that there is coverage for any other business if underlying coverage is in place. Therefore, a home-based business cannot be presumed to have personal liability coverage under the personal umbrella; coverage must be added by means of endorsement. DL 98 05 02 15 personal umbrella liability policy excess business pursuits coverage endorsement, and DL 98 03 02 15 personal umbrella liability policy excess home business liability coverage endorsement may be attached.

Before leaving the topic of business, we note that the three forms all exclude coverage for any professional services undertaken by an insured. In the MSO form this is exclusion 16, in the AAIS, exclusion 2, and in the ISO, exclusion 6.

Care, Custody and Control

We touched on this exclusion somewhat in Chapter 5, "Recreational Vehicles", when we noted that both the AAIS and ISO homeowners forms, under liability coverage for damage to property of others, allowed up to $1,000 for a nonowned recreational motor vehicle. However, a true umbrella policy responds to an insured's liability for property in his or her care, custody, or control.

In this regard, the MSO umbrella form is lacking. There are two exclusions pertaining to property in an insured's custody; the first, exclusion 11. nonowned property exclusion, declares the insurer will "not cover property damage to property in the care of, occupied or used by, or rented to, any insured." (The MSO homeowners policy, however, covers property damage to a nonowned premises occupied by, rented to, or in the care of an insured for the perils of smoke, fire, and explosion). The second exclusion, though not strictly thought of as "care, custody and control," has to do with property owned by an insured. The umbrella's exclusion 13. eliminates coverage for property damage to property owned by any insured. The two exclusions —11. and 13.—are both in the umbrella.

The ISO umbrella form, in exclusion 18., states there is no coverage for "'property damage' to property rented to, occupied or used by, or in the care, custody or control of, an 'insured' to the extent that the 'insured' is obligated by contract to provide insurance for such property. However, this exclusion (A.18) does not apply to 'property damage' caused by fire, smoke or explosion." What the exclusion is stating is that if there is a contract that the insured provide insurance for property in his or her care, then the insurer will only provide coverage for damage done by fire, smoke, or explosion. However, in all other cases, the umbrella will drop down to provide coverage. Coverage is thus broader than in the MSO umbrella. Like the MSO form, though, the ISO umbrella also excludes coverage for "'property damage' to property owned by an 'insured'. This includes costs or expenses incurred by an 'insured' or others to repair, replace, enhance, restore or maintain such property to prevent injury to a person or damage to property of others, whether on or away from the residence premises shown in the Declarations."

A word of explanation: the exclusions for damage to owned property arose from the case of *Aetna Ins. Co. v. Aaron*, 685 A.2d 858 (Md. Ct. Spec. App. 1996), in which the court held that the costs of measures the association took to repair the insured's condominium in order to prevent further damage to a neighboring condominium were potentially a part of property damage liability. The court said the owned property exclusion (as then written) did not apply, because a third party's property sustained the damage.

The AAIS umbrella form has no exclusion for property rented to, occupied by, or otherwise in the care of an insured. Although the form may be relying on the underlying homeowners exclusion of coverage except for damage caused by smoke, fire, or explosion, the more likely explanation is that the umbrella is fulfilling its function of "dropping down" in true umbrella style to provide necessary coverage, since there is no applicable exclusion. But like the ISO and MSO umbrellas, the AAIS umbrella exclusion for owned property (31.) states that there is no coverage for "'property damage' to property owned by an 'insured'. This exclusion also applies to cost or expense for measures performed on property owned by an 'insured' to prevent: a. injury to a person; or b. damage to property of others; on or away from an 'insured premises', whether such cost or expense is incurred by an 'insured' or others." So, if an insured has a condo in a gothic-style building, and his favorite gargoyle is in danger of falling onto passers-by below, the cost to remove the gargoyle will not be covered.

Intentional Acts

Homeowners forms exclude bodily injury or property damage intentionally caused. The current (09 08) AAIS homeowners form excludes:

"bodily injury" or "property damage" that is:

1) expected by, directed by, or intended by an "insured";
2) the result of a criminal act of an "insured"; or
3) the result of an intentional and malicious act by or at the direction of an "insured".

This exclusion applies even if the "bodily injury" or "property damage":

1) that occurs is different than what was expected, directed, or intended; or
2) is suffered by persons, entities, or property not expected, directed, or intended.

However, this exclusion does not apply to bodily injury or property damage that arises out of the use of reasonable force to protect people or property.

The current ISO homeowners (05 11) is substantially the same, except that it does not refer to bodily injury or property damage that is the result of a criminal act. The MSO homeowners form (01 11) excludes coverage for: "*bodily injury* or *property damage*, whether or not expected or intended, that is a consequence of an *insured's* willfully harmful act or knowing endangerment." There is no exception, as in the ISO and AAIS forms, for actions taken to protect persons or property.

The MSO umbrella's exclusion is similar to the homeowner's, but a few more items are added. There is no coverage for bodily injury or property damage, whether or not expected or intended by the insured:

A. Which is a consequence of an *insured's* willfully harmful act or knowing endangerment;

B. Which arises out of the transmission of a communicable disease by an *insured*; or

C. Which arises out of sexual molestation, corporal punishment, or physical or mental abuse.

Now, this is not to say that the ISO and AAIS forms cover the latter two actions—they do not. The exclusions are not found under the intentional acts exclusion, and will be discussed below.

The AAIS umbrella utilizes the same wording as in the homeowners; however, the following wording is added:

> There is no coverage for anyone who is an "insured" under this policy for any "bodily injury" or "property damage" arising out of any of the acts described in a., b., or c. [1., 2., and 3. in the homeowners] above regardless of the theory of relief pursued, asserted, or claimed against the person or entity seeking coverage under this policy.

This language is designed to prevent a suit based, say, on negligent supervision when, as happened in a case we will look at, the plaintiff claimed parents did not properly hide a gun from their son. The AAIS form continues:

> This exclusion applies even if the "bodily injury"' or "property damage" that occurs is different than what was expected, directed, or intended or is suffered by persons, entities, or property not expected, directed, or intended.

The ISO 05 11 homeowners form declares there is no coverage for:

> "Bodily injury" or "property damage" which is expected or intended by an "insured", even if the resulting "bodily injury" or "property damage":
>
> a. Is of a different kind, quality or degree than initially expected or intended; or
>
> b. Is sustained by a different person, entity or property than initially expected or intended.

However, this exclusion E.1. does not apply to "bodily injury" or "property damage" resulting from the use of reasonable force by an "insured" to protect persons or property.

The ISO umbrella form's exclusion is nearly the same as the homeowner's; however, there is another exception:

> ...this exclusion (A.1.) does not apply to:

(2) "bodily injury" or "property damage" resulting from the use of reasonable force by an "insured" to prevent or eliminate danger in the operation of "autos", "recreational motor vehicles" or watercraft.

Thus, the exclusion would not apply if, for example, an insured grabbed the steering wheel of a car whose driver had suddenly collapsed, and, in so doing, drove the car into the highway guard rail and away from on-coming traffic.

Before continuing our discussion of other exclusions that conceivably fall into the "intentional act" camp, let's take a look at some judicial thinking.

We mentioned above the case involving a "hidden gun." Actually, the gun had not been hidden by his parents at all—the son illegally purchased it. He and several friends were partying with beer, Xanax, and marijuana. They spent the day at the beach, and then returned to the son's parents' house, where they continued the party in the garage. Osvaldo, the son, got out a gun he'd illegally purchased and started to waive it around, showing it off. He put it away, but got it out later to show more friends. Another friend took the gun and saw it was loaded, but could not remember later if the safety had been on. He gave the gun back to Osvaldo; it went off, and Holly Hieber was fatally wounded. Her mother brought suit against Osvaldo and his parents, alleging they had negligently hidden the gun. In the meantime, Osvaldo was charged with involuntary manslaughter, which served to bar coverage under the policy. The exclusion was similar to those given above, with these two differences. First, the exclusion "applies even if such insured person lacks the mental capacity to govern his or her conduct." Second, the exclusion "applies regardless of whether or not such insured person is actually charged with, or convicted of a crime." So, in the case of *Allstate Indemnity Company v. Hieber*, 24 N.E.3d 139 (Ill. App. 2014), no coverage.

Sometimes when it appears clear-cut that the exclusion will apply, though, the court will find it does not. In the case of *Allstate Insurance Company et al. v. Campbell et al.*, 942 N.E.2d 1090 (Oh. 2010), the court applied the doctrine of inferred intent (the insured's intentional act and the harm caused are intrinsically tied so that the act has necessarily resulted in the harm) to find that three of four pranksters were entitled to coverage when they put a target deer, made of styrofoam, in the middle of a road. An oncoming driver swerved to avoid the "deer," and wound up in a ditch. He and his passenger were injured. The court found coverage for three of the pranksters, but not the fourth, stating that in his case the exclusion clearly applied.

This next case, also heard by the Ohio Supreme Court, differed with regard to the doctrine. In *Lachman et al. v. Farmers Insurance of Columbus*, 2012 WL 112637 (Oh. 2012) the court applied the same doctrine, and held the insured was not entitled to coverage when her house burned down, along with a portion of her neighbor's. She intentionally set fire to a comforter in a bedroom in attempt to "make her husband look heroic." Even though she did not intend the fire to spread, the results of setting a fire were reasonably foreseeable. So, no coverage.

Let's take a look at some exclusions that preclude coverage for actions that are intentional, although they are listed separately.

In the ISO form, exclusion 15. eliminates coverage for "bodily injury" or "personal injury" arising out of:

a. The transmission of a communicable disease by an "insured";

b. Sexual molestation, corporal punishment or physical or mental abuse; or

c. The use, sale, manufacture, delivery, transfer or possession by any person of a Controlled Substance(s) as defined by the Federal Food and Drug Law at 21 U.S.C.A. Sections 811 and 812. Controlled Substances include but are not limited to cocaine, LSD, marijuana and all narcotic drugs. However, this exclusion (A.15) does not apply to the legitimate use of prescription drugs by a person following the lawful orders of a licensed health care professional.

Note that despite some state laws to the contrary, certain drugs are still considered controlled substances, and the umbrella form is quite clear as to the lack of coverage if there is abuse.

The MSO umbrella form exclusion 8.A.5. also eliminates coverage for any drug-related activities, other than those legitimately prescribed by a "licensed physician." (Note the difference here—a licensed physician is different from a "licensed health care professional," which might be a nurse practitioner. Exclusion 8.A.4. precludes coverage for "knowing violation of penal law or ordinance committed by, or with the consent of, an 'insured'."

The AAIS form also contains exclusions for the same actions; however, the AAIS form also excludes coverage for "property damage" arising from them. These are exclusions 5, 6, 7, 8, and 9. Additionally, the AAIS form, following the exclusion for injury arising out of the use of controlled substances, adds: "However, this exclusion does not apply to the extent that such "bodily injury", "personal injury", or "property damage" is covered by "underlying insurance" at the time of the "occurrence" or offense or would have been covered but for the exhaustion of its "limits". It is possible that the AAIS form is allowing for the possibility of coverage if the underlying homeowners form allows for someone to grow a limited number of pot plants for sale; however, at present, no instances of this were found.

The Intrafamily Exclusion

Homeowners forms commonly exclude coverage for bodily injury to one insured family member caused by another insured family member. This exclusion of coverage is often called the intrafamily exclusion. There are three reasons for this exclusion. One is that such claims disturb domestic harmony; the second is that it places an unfair burden on the insurer to determine if there has been collusion; the third is that the policy was never intended to replace medical coverage. Therefore, the ISO homeowners forms state:

> Coverage E – Personal Liability, does not apply to… bodily injury to you or an insured as defined under Definition 5.a. or b.
>
> This exclusion also applies to any claim made or suit brought against you or an "insured" to:
>
> a. Repay; or
>
> b. Share damages with;
>
> another person who may be obligated to pay damages because of "bodily injury" to an "insured".

The AAIS form is similar in that there is no coverage for bodily injury to an insured as defined, nor is there coverage for any claim or suit seeking participation in damages for which another person is liable.

The MSO homeowners form declares there is no coverage for *bodily injury* to any *insured* under Part A of the definition of *insureds*. The form is silent, though, with regard to an exclusion baring coverage for a claim or suit seeking participation in damages. To see how this latter works, we look at the case of *American Family Mutual Insurance Company v. Tamala Jo Ryan et al.*, 330 N.W.2d 113 (Minnesota 1983). Tamala Jo, age three, was playing in a neighbor's yard. Her mother was also in the yard working in a garden shared by the two families. The neighbor was mowing his grass using a riding lawn mower, and somehow Tamala Jo fell so that the blades severely damaged her foot and ankle, with the result that she had to have her leg amputated. The Ryans sued the lawn mower manufacturer, who sued them in return alleging negligent supervision and seeking contribution or indemnity. The insureds tendered their defense to their insurer, American Family.

Relying on the exclusion for bodily injury to an insured or to a resident relative of the insured, American Family denied coverage. The case went to the state supreme court, which affirmed that the Minnesota statutes did not prohibit such exclusions, and therefore the household exclusion was valid.

The intrafamily exclusion appears in the personal auto policy (PAP) by endorsement in the states where it is allowed. For example, Ohio's endorsement PP 01 86 09 13 states that there is no liability coverage "for any 'insured' for 'bodily injury' to you or any 'family member'. However, this exclusion does not apply to a wrongful death action brought against an 'insured'." The amendatory endorsement (PP 01 60 10 13) of Minnesota states that the insurer will "not provide 'bodily injury' to you or a family member to the extent that the limits of liability for this coverage exceed the Minnesota limits of liability required by the financial responsibility law of Minnesota". There is no consistency; however, where the exclusion exists, it has generally been upheld.

Umbrella forms generally are as one in excluding bodily injury or personal injury to an insured. The MSO form, in exclusion 9., precludes coverage for *bodily injury* or *personal injury* to any *insured*. The ISO exclusion (14.) is for "bodily injury" or "personal injury" to you or a "family member". The exclusion also applies to a suit or claim to share damages with another person who may be obligated to pay damages because of injury to an insured. The AAIS form differs somewhat from the others, though not in what is excluded. Rather, in AAIS exclusion 12. there is a reference to the exclusion's also applying to a "household member." Now, a "household member" means, as one would expect, resident relatives, relatives under age twenty-five and in school full time, etc. However, this is added:

e. an "insured, other than a person described in a. through d. above, who:

   1) lives with "you";

   2) is a member of "your" household; and

   3) is not a guest, "domestic employee", "employee", tenant, or roomer or boarder; and

f. an "insured" under the age of twenty-one years, other than a person described in a. through d. above, who lives with and is in the legal custody of a person described in e. above.

This language would eliminate coverage for "bodily injury" to an unmarried live-in partner or girl- or boyfriend. Additionally, if the live-in partner or friend had children in his or her legal custody, the exclusion would also apply to them. Spelling this out prevents much action in a court of law to determine just how the exclusion is to be applied.

Let's take a look at how the courts have viewed this exclusion, before moving into the wacky world of "personal injury," and all the weird, wonderful, and wordy exclusions the use of the internet has brought to the personal umbrella.

First, a case in Kentucky, where the exclusion was not upheld. Larry Marley was driving from Indiana to Florida, and fell asleep at the wheel in Kentucky, killing one daughter and injuring his wife, son and another daughter. The wife sued on behalf of her son, daughter and deceased daughter, citing negligence. The suit was brought in Kentucky, since that was the scene of the accident. The circuit court upheld the household exclusion; the appellate court reversed, and the Supreme Court had the final say. The court found the exclusion in the umbrella policy was void and against public policy as it applied to automobile coverage (*State Farm Mutual Automobile Insurance Company v. Marley* et al., 151 S.W.3d 33 [Ky. 2004]).

Second, a case in Montana, where the court looked at *Marley*, and said that, if insurers were to provide umbrella coverage to the extent that household members were to be compensated for their injuries at the hand of another insured, coverage would become unaffordable. The court held that the exclusion that eliminated coverage when a wife sued her husband for negligent driving prevented "suspect interfamily legal actions, which may not be truly adversary and over which insurer would have little to no control." The court said that Kentucky's lack of distinction between mandatory (as in the mandatory auto insurance laws) and optional coverage (the umbrella) was irrelevant, and Kentucky's statement that the exclusion was "arbitrary" was for "no legitimate reason" (*McCartney v. State Farm Mutual Automobile Insurance Company*, 305 P.3d 861 (Mont. 2013).

Finally, the exclusion has been upheld in *Khandelwal v. Zurich Insurance Co.*, et al., 50 A.3d 52 (N.J. Super. 2012), *Bjork v. State Farm Fire and Casualty et al.* (157 Cal. App 4th, 2007), and *Hoque v. Empire Fire and Marine Ins. Co.*, 637 S.E.2d 465 (Geo. App. 2006), among others. The first two cases involved the auto policy and the umbrella; the last homeowners and the umbrella. But in the case of *Fortunato v. Highlands Ins. Group, et al.*, 785 A.2d 963 (N.J. Super 2001), the homeowners policy excluded bodily injury to a named insured, but the umbrella did not. Therefore, there was coverage under the umbrella for a judgment against the husband being negligent in not removing ice and snow on the steps of their home, causing his wife to fall.

Chapter 7

Exclusions: Part II

Introduction

In this chapter we will examine the exclusions for personal injury, pollution and pollutants, war, workers compensation, and several miscellaneous exclusions—some of which do not appear with any regularity in the forms.

Personal Injury

Next we take a look at the exclusions for personal injury. Many of the exclusions we will review were unforeseen in the earlier editions of the personal umbrella. For example, in the AAIS 01 00 edition, which was reprinted in the 2000 edition of this book, the number of pages was eleven. But now, the 10 11 edition numbers some sixteen pages. And although we cannot say that this is entirely due to an increase in personal injury exclusions, we now have twenty exclusions specifically referencing personal injury as opposed to eleven. Many of the exclusions we will examine include "property damage" and "bodily injury" as well as "personal injury"' however, the thrust of many of them is damage caused by use the internet, Facebook, Twitter, Spotify, Instagram, etc.

"Personal injury" was defined in Chapter Two, "Definitions", and in this Chapter we have already reviewed the exclusion for "personal injury" arising out of a business or an intentional act. Note that many times the exclusions are not strictly for "personal injury," but include "bodily injury" and "property damage" as well. Often the reason for this is to prevent the possibility that a claimant will say, for example, "Well, the transmission of a communicable disease did not hurt me physically, but slandered my reputation." Other exclusions including "personal injury" will be dealt with in the section on Pollution.

The MSO exclusions are:

4. We do not cover *bodily injury*, *property damage* or *personal injury* arising out of or resulting from electronic aggression.

8.A.3. Violation of any ordinance, regulation or statute that prohibits or limits the communicating, distributing, sending or transmitting of material or information such as the Telephone Consumer Protection Act (TCPA) or the CAN-SPAM Act of 2003, including any amendments or additions to such laws.

14. We do not cover any *personal injury*:

   A. Arising out of oral or written publication of material, if done by or at the direction of the insured with knowledge of its falsity; or

   B. Arising out of oral or written publication of material whose first publication took place before the beginning of the policy period. All personal injury arising out of publication of the same or similar material subsequent to the beginning of the policy period is also excluded.

Exclusion 4. is targeted specifically at internet use, while exclusions 14.A. and 14.B. have been common in umbrellas for several years. Exclusion 8.A.3 relates more to a business; however, it is conceivable someone might decide to use his or her personal phone to solicit business, or personal computer to send commercial email and so the umbrella denies coverage.

The ISO umbrella form eliminates coverage for "personal injury":

2. a. Caused by or at the direction of an "insured" with the knowledge that the act would violate the rights of another and would inflict "personal injury";

   b. Arising out of oral or written publication of material, if done by or at the direction of an "insured" with knowledge or its falsity;

[Refer to the case of *Giustibelli* in Chapter 2 to see this exclusion in action.]

   c. Arising out of oral or written publication of material whose first publication took place before the beginning of the policy period;

   d. Arising out of a criminal act committed by or at the direction of an "insured"; or

   e. Sustained by any person as a result of an offense directly or indirectly related to the employment of this person by an "insured".

This latter exclusion explains the exclusion for "personal injury" with regard to the "business" exclusions. For example, a company owner might constantly berate an employee, with comments to the effect that he or she is stupid, incompetent, etc. If the insurer relied strictly on the "business" exclusion (without including "personal injury") then the claimant could say the remarks were not "business" related. So, if the offense also appears as a personal injury exclusion, the policy has made it clear that, no matter the argument presented, there will be no coverage. The exclusion can also refer to, say, a domestic employee of an insured; the operative words being "the employment of this person *by* [italics added] an 'insured'."

We now turn to the AAIS exclusions (that is, those in addition to those already discussed). There is no coverage for:

10. "bodily injury", "personal injury", or "property damage" that arises out of electronic aggression, including but not limited to harassment or bullying committed:

    a. by means of an electronic forum, including but not limited to a blog, an electronic chat room, a gripe site, a social networking site, a web site, or a weblog; or

    b. by other electronic means, including but not limited to email, instant messaging, or text messaging.

AAIS also eliminates coverage for "bodily injury", "personal injury", or "property damage "arising directly or indirectly from the TCPA or CAN-SPAM Act, and also from any federal, state, or local law, ordinance, statute, or regulation other than these that limits or prohibits transmitting of material or information.

Like ISO, AAIS precludes coverage for "'personal injury' sustained by any person as a result of an offense directly or indirectly related to such person's employment by an 'insured', or leasing by an 'insured' under a contract or an agreement with a labor leasing firm (25.). Additionally, AAIS excludes coverage for:

24. "personal injury" arising out of an act committed by or directed by an "insured" who knew that the act would violate the rights of another and would result in "personal injury".

26. "personal injury" arising out of oral or written publication, including electronic publication, or material that was first published before the effective date of this insurance.

27. "personal injury" arising out of oral or written publication, including electronic publication, of material by or at the direction of an "insured" who knew that the publication was false.

29. "personal injury" arising out of a criminal act committed by or directed by an "insured".

30. "personal injury" arising out of electronic chat rooms, bulletin boards, gripe sites, social networking sites, or other forums that an "insured" hosts, owns, or has the control or authority to update.

However, this exclusion does not apply to "personal injury" arising out of content posted by an "insured" or provided by an "insured" for posting by others to a web site, weblog, blog, or other electronic forum.

These exclusions have been added since the internet gained such control over our lives. Let's take another look at how the courts have reacted to these exclusions. We already noted, in Chapter 2, how an online rant can have an adverse reaction (*Giustibelli*). There is still some free-speech protection, however, as seen in the case of *Neumann et al. v. Liles*, 2016 WL 852812 (Ore. 2016). Liles was a guest at a wedding held on Neumann's property (Dancing Deer Mountain, LLC, a wedding site). Two days later he posted a review, using many exclamation marks, about the disastrous day, saying, among other things, "There are many other great places to get married, this is not that place! The worst wedding experience of my life!" Neumann sued for defamation, but the Oregon Supreme Court upheld Liles's comments, using a three-pronged test: (1) the statement's broad context, which includes the general tenor of the entire work; (2) the specific context and content of the statements, and the reasonable expectations of the audience in that particular situation; and (3) whether the statement itself is sufficiently factual to be susceptible of being proved true or false. In this case the court felt that a reasonable reader would interpret the comments as being those of a single unhappy guest, and not a presentation of objective facts. The court noted the (over)use of exclamation marks in support of its findings.

Oregon, we should note, has an anti-SLAPP statute (strategic litigation against public participation), which is a statute designed to discourage lawsuits initiated to chill discussion on matters of public interest. So, before writing any online review, either use lots of exclamation marks or make sure your state has an anti-SLAPP statute.

This next case involves personal injury; we include it because the definition of "personal injury" differs from the three we have been discussing: "'Personal injury' means: a. bodily injury, sickness or disease, disability or shock including required care, loss of services and death resulting therefrom; b. mental anguish or mental injury…" In *Safeco Insurance Company of America v. Vecsey*, 2010 WL 3925126 (U.S. Dist. Conn. 2010), the court found that the exclusions for bodily injury arising out of abuse, out of intended acts, and for bodily injury to an insured precluded coverage under both the homeowners and umbrella policies for Roderick Vecsey for injury suffered by his wife when he threw a carrot at her and injured her eye.

Finally, ShaqAttack! Binion sued Shaquille O'Neal for invasion of privacy, alleging he posted mocking pictures of him on social media websites. The court found for O'Neal, because the suit was brought in Michigan but O'Neal had, said the court, millions of followers worldwide. Therefore, the defendant did not have a substantial connection with the "forum" state, i.e., Michigan. This case is *Binion v. O'Neal et al.*, 95 F.Supp. 3d 1055 (U.S. Dist. Mi. 2015). We should point out that this case does not demonstrate that posting nasty photos on a web site is acceptable and will be overlooked by the courts—quite the opposite. Most people do not have a fan-base of millions, and so what might be overlooked in a celebrity (even given the time and money spent in a defense) will not be overlooked in the average person.

As an agent, it might be wise to regularly remind clients—particularly those with children—that what might appear to be a prank (name-calling on Facebook, Snapchat, etc.) could have far-reaching consequences. One insurer has rolled out "cyber-bully" coverage; that is, coverage for time and effort restoring a damaged reputation, but of course that will not aid the initiator of the bullying.

Pollution and Pollutants

Let's leave personal injury and move on to the umbrella's exclusions for pollution and pollutants. We are including fungi within this category since, although naturally-occurring (unlike, say, pollutants which are normally thought of as man-made in origin) similar exclusions apply. The first edition (2000) of this book contained few such exclusions, since they were not so common. Today, although the unendorsed homeowners forms may not have exclusions for liability arising out of pollutants, often endorsements precluding coverage are added by the insurers. Although both the AAIS and the ISO basic homeowners forms do not exclude liability coverage for bodily injury or property damage arising out of pollution or lead contamination, insurers are increasingly apt to attach exclusions. For example, ISO has developed an endorsement that gives limited lead and escaped liquid fuel liability coverage (HO 05 80; form number varies by state). This endorsement illustrates the two areas of major concern to insurers: liability arising out of the ingestion or inhalation of lead, and liability arising out of liquid fuel polluting neighboring premises and ground water. The MSO homeowners forms exclude liability coverage for any cleanup etc., of fuel oil.

We'll start with the MSO umbrella form, which is the strictest in eliminating coverage for damage or injury done by pollutants.

MSO defines *fungi* as "any type or form of fungus, mold, mildew, spores, algae, smut, protists, rusts or *rot and decay organisms*, and any similar or related organisms and any mycotoxin, substance, compounds, chemicals, mist or vapor produced by any *fungi* in any form, or any by-products or waste produced by *fungi*, but does not include any *fungi* intended to be edible. *Rot and decay organisms* means any living organism that causes decomposition of physical property." *Pollutants* are "any gaseous, liquid, solid, or thermal contaminant or irritant, including acids, alkalis, chemicals, fumes, smoke, soot, vapors, and waste (including materials to be reclaimed, reconditioned, or recycled)." Finally, the MSO form includes definitions for lead-based paint and lead-based paint hazard: "*lead-based paint* means paint or other surface coatings that contain lead equal to or in excess of 1.0 milligram per square centimeter or 0.5 percent by weight. *Lead-based paint hazard* means any condition that causes exposure to lead from lead-contaminated dust, lead-contaminated soil, or lead-contaminated paint that is deteriorated or present in accessible surfaces, friction surfaces, or impact surfaces that would result in adverse human health effects as established by the appropriate Federal agency." *Asbestos* means "the mineral in any form, including but not limited to fibers or dust."

Predictably, the MSO umbrella comprehensively excludes coverage for:

15.A. ...*bodily injury, property damage* or *personal injury* arising out of, caused by, or resulting from any of the following:

1. The actual, alleged, or threatened discharge, dispersal, emission, escape, flowing, leakage, migration, release, or seepage of pollutants or other similar forms of environmental damage, regardless of where or how such may take place.
2. The actual, alleged, or threatened exposure to asbestos; or the presence of asbestos in any place.
3. Lead or lead contamination. This includes injury or damage caused by or through absorbing lead, chewing on, eating or otherwise ingesting lead or inhaling lead; or the contamination of, or existence of, lead in air, ground or water, or any part of a premises including, but not limited to, building materials and paint.

15.B. ....any cost, expense, liability, or loss rising out of any of the following:

1. Any demand, directive, order, or request that any *insured* or others clean up, contain, detoxify, monitor, neutralize,

remove, test for, treat, or in any way assess the effects of or respond to *pollutants, asbestos*, lead or lead contamination; or

2. Any claim or suit by, or on behalf of, any governmental authority for damages or reimbursement because of cleaning up, containing, detoxifying, monitoring, neutralizing, removing, testing for, treating, or in any way assessing the effects of or responding to *pollutants, asbestos*, lead or lead contamination.

The form goes on to state that there is no coverage should an insured fail to disclose the presence of lead-based paint or a lead-based paint hazard at the time of a sale or lease of a residential building, nor will the insurer defend any suit regarding the same.

Note that this exclusion, as well as the exclusions we will discuss in the AAIS and ISO forms, include "personal injury" among the items not covered. The reason for this is that "personal injury" usually includes within its definition "wrongful entry" of property. Since many contaminants migrate from real property to real property, the inclusion of "wrongful entry" clarifies that a suit alleging wrongful entry of pollutants (as from a propane tank on an insured's property) onto the real property of another will not be covered.

Having mentioned propane, we see the MSO exclusion for fuel oil precludes coverage for:

6.A. ...property damage arising out of the actual or threatened discharge, dispersal, disposal, emission, escape, flowing, leaching, leakage, migration, release, seepage or spill of fuel oil regardless of where or how such may take place.

Continuing exclusion 6., the insurer will not cover any cost, expense, liability, or loss arising out of any of the following:

B.1. Any demand, directive, order, or request that any insured or others clean up, contain, detoxify, monitor, neutralize, remove, test for, treat, or in any way assess the effects of or respond to fuel oil or fuel oil contamination; or

B.2. Any claim or suit by, or on behalf of, any governmental authority for damages or reimbursement because of cleaning up, containing, detoxifying, monitoring, neutralizing, removing, testing for, treating, or in any way assessing the effects of or responding to fuel oil or fuel oil contamination.

The exclusion for damage caused by fuel oil is similar to that found in many homeowners forms for pollutants—however, in the homeowners forms the exclusions are typically found in the property coverages, and not in the liability section. For example, in the ISO HO 00 03, under the exclusion for Ordinance or Law, the form states there is no coverage for a loss requiring "any insured to test for, monitor, clean up, remove, contain, treat, detoxify … or in any way respond to, or assess the effects of, pollutants." (The release of pollutants onto insured property is covered if caused by a coverage C named peril.) However, the MSO homeowners form contains a liability exclusion identical to that of the umbrella form; namely, that the insurer will not pay for any property damage caused by fuel oil.

Continuing with the MSO umbrella form, we find the exclusion for *fungi* and mold:

A. We do not cover *bodily injury* or *property damage*, resulting from or caused by the actual, alleged, or threatened absorption of, contact with, existence of, exposure to, inhalation of, ingestion of, or presence of any *fungi*.

B. We do not cover any cost, expense, liability or loss arising out of any of the following;

   1. Any demand, directive, order, or request that any insured or others clean up, contain, detoxify, monitor, neutralize, remove, test for, or treat, or in any way assess the effects of or respond to *fungi*.

   2. Any claim or suit by, or on behalf of, any governmental authority for damages or reimbursement because of cleaning up, containing, detoxifying, monitoring, neutralizing, removing, testing for, treating, or in any way assessing the effects of or responding to *fungi*.

However, these exclusions do not apply to bodily injury resulting from the ingestion of foods, goods or products intended for human consumption.

As we will see, the exclusions for damage done by pollutants are much less stringent in the ISO and AAIS umbrella forms. Further, the ISO and AAIS homeowners forms do not have liability exclusions governing the release or escape of fuel oil, let alone other pollutants. That is not to say that the umbrellas follow form and grant coverage for such occurrences; they do not. However, the pollutants exclusions are not so numerous.

First, the ISO definition of a "fuel system":

I. "Fuel system" means:

   1. One or more containers, tanks or vessels which have a total combined storage capacity of 100 or more U.S. gallons of liquid fuel; and:

a. Are, or were, located on any single location covered by "underlying insurance"; and

b. Are, or were, used to hold liquid fuel that is intended to be used solely for one or more of the following:

(1) To heat or cool a building;

(2) To heat water;

(3) To cook food; or

(4) To power motor vehicles, other motorized land conveyances or watercraft owned by an "insured";

2. Any pumping apparatus, which includes the motor, gauge, nozzle, hose or pipes that are, or were, connected to one or more containers, tanks or vessels described in Paragraph I.1.;

3. Filler pipes and flues connected to one or more containers, tanks or vessels described in Paragraph I.1.;

4. A boiler, furnace or a water heater, the liquid fuel for which is stored in a container, tank or vessel described in Paragraph I.1.;

5. Fittings and pipes connecting the boiler, furnace or water heater to one or more containers, tanks or vessels described in Paragraph I.1.; or

6. A structure that is specifically designed and built to hold the liquid fuel that escapes from one or more containers, tanks or vessels described in Paragraph I.1.

The reason for this lengthy definition for a fuel system lies in exclusion 21., which eliminates coverage for "bodily injury", "personal injury" or "property damage" caused by an "occurrence" or offense involving the escape of fuel from a "fuel system." Remember, "personal injury" is included so it cannot be argued that the fuel wrongfully entered the property of another. (The ISO homeowners forms have no similar exclusion.)

The remaining ISO exclusions for any kind of pollutants are:

22. "Bodily injury" or "personal injury" caused by an "occurrence" or offense involving the absorption, ingestion or inhalation of lead; or

23. "Personal injury" or "property damage" caused by an "occurrence or offense of lead contamination.

Although the ISO form does not contain an exclusion for loss resulting from fungi, an endorsement to eliminate coverage may be added (DL 98 17 02 15). The ISO homeowners forms do not exclude bodily injury or property damage caused by lead, but remember that umbrellas can cover rental property liability, and so the insurer will not want to provide coverage for something a landlord should take care of.

Next, we'll look at the AAIS exclusions. The AAIS form defines *fungi*, as well as *pollutant*. Fungi means "any kind or form of fungus, including but not limited to mildew and mold, and any chemical, matter, or compound produced or released by a fungus, including but not limited to toxins, spores, fragments, and metabolites such as microbial volatile organic compounds." A pollutant is:

a. any solid, liquid, gaseous, thermal, or radioactive irritant or contaminant, including acids, alkalis, chemicals, fumes, smoke, soot, vapor, and waste. Waste includes materials to be disposed of as well as recycled, reclaimed, or reconditioned; and

b. electrical, magnetic, or electromagnetic particles or fields, whether visible or invisible, and sound.

The AAIS umbrella form, as well as the AAIS homeowners forms, treat electromagnetic waves, etc., as pollutants—just something to be aware of. Sound is also considered a pollutant, so a reminder to parents of party-loving teenagers might be in order.

The AAIS form precludes coverage for:

4. "bodily injury", "personal injury", or "property damage" that arises out of the actual, alleged, or threatened discharge, dispersal, disposal, emission, escape, leaching, leakage, migration, release, seepage, or spillage of "pollutants" into or upon land, water, or air.

However, this exclusion does not apply to:

a. "bodily injury" or "property damage" that arises out of the heat, smoke, or fumes of a fire on an "insured premises" that becomes uncontrollable or breaks out from where it was intended to be; or

b. "bodily injury" or "property damage" that arises out of the actual, alleged, or threatened discharge, dispersal, disposal, emission, escape, leaching, leakage, migration, release, seepage, or spillage of "pollutants" from a "motorized vehicle", but only to the extent that such "bodily injury" or "property damage" is covered by "underlying insurance" at the time of the "occurrence" or would have been covered but for the exhaustion of its "limits".

Unlike the MSO form, which considered smoke and soot pollutants, the AAIS form, in an exception to the pollutants exclusion, gives back coverage for loss arising out of an uncontrollable fire on the insured premises, or from a motor vehicle, provided there is underlying coverage. So, if an insured is legally burning brush in an oil can on his own property, and the fire escapes its confines and puts out smoke and soot, a suit alleging property damage would be covered.

The AAIS form eliminates coverage for:

21. actual or alleged "bodily injury" that arises directly or indirectly out of the ingestion, inhalation, or absorption of lead in any form.

23. "personal injury" arising out of lead in any form.

28. "personal injury" arising directly or indirectly, in whole or in part, from the actual, alleged, or threatened ingestion of, inhalation of, contact with, exposure to, existence of, presence of, or any activity of bacteria, "fungi", wet rot, or dry rot.

32. actual or alleged "property damage" that arises directly or indirectly out of any form of lead.

36. any loss, cost, or expense arising out of any:

    a. request, demand, order, or statutory or regulatory requirement that an "insured" or others test for, monitor, clean up, remove, contain, treat, detoxify, neutralize, or in any way respond to or assess the effects of "pollutants"' or

    b. claim or suit by or on behalf of any governmental body or authority relating to testing from monitoring, cleaning up, removing, containing, treating, detoxifying, neutralizing, or in any way responding to or assessing the effects of "pollutants".

However, this exclusion does not apply to such loss, cost, or expense arising out of a "motorized vehicle", but only to the extent that the loss, cost, or expense is covered by "underlying insurance" at the time of the "occurrence" or would have been but for the exhaustion of its "limits".

37. any loss, cost, or expense arising out of any:

    a. request, demand, order, or statutory or regulatory requirement that an "insured" or others test for, monitor, clean up, remove, contain, treat, detoxify, neutralize, or in any way respond to or assess the effects of lead; or

    b. claim or suit by or on behalf of any governmental body or authority relating to testing for, monitoring, cleaning up, removing, containing, treating, detoxifying, neutralizing, or in any way responding to or assessing the effects of lead.

38. loss, cost, or expense arising out of any:

    a. request, demand, order, or statutory or regulatory requirement that an "insured" or others test for, monitor, clean up, remove, contain, treat, detoxify, neutralize, or in any way respond to or assess the effects of bacteria, "fungi", wet rot, or dry rot; or

    b. claim or suit by or on behalf of any governmental body or authority relating to testing for, monitoring, cleaning up, removing, containing, treating, detoxifying, neutralizing, or in any way responding to or assessing the effects of bacteria, "fungi", wet rot, or dry rot.

That concludes the lengthy list of exclusions for pollution, pollutants, etc. Note that the AAIS exclusions give coverage for any fuel oil spillage from a "motorized vehicle" provided there is underlying coverage. So, if a condo resident parked in his or her garage, and the car developed a leak from the fuel tank so that neighboring property was damaged, there would be coverage if the local governmental authority demanded a cleanup. It might be that the AAIS form contains this great number of exclusions for pollutants such as wet rot, lead, and other polluting agents because the AAIS eligibility requirements allow the umbrella to be written over a business such as a bed and breakfast, or a farm—that is, provided the insurer agrees. If that is the case, it is probable that an insurer would not wish a personal umbrella to insure liability arising out of a release of farm pollutants.

War and Nuclear Exclusions

The three umbrella forms all have exclusions relating to war and nuclear energy. MSO excludes coverage for "any act or condition of war (declared or not), civil war, invasion, insurrection, rebellion, revolution, or seizure of power, including acts done to defend against such acts or conditions, whether actual or expected." The ISO exclusion (11.) for war is similar, but the exclusion concludes with "Discharge of a nuclear weapon will be deemed a warlike act even if accidental." The AAIS exclusion for war (19.) mirrors the ISO exclusion.

With regard to exclusions for nuclear occurrences, the AAIS form eliminates coverage for "'bodily injury' or 'property damage' arising out of an "occurrence" for which an "insured" is also an insured under a nuclear energy liability policy or would be an insured under a nuclear energy liability policy but for the exhaustion of its "limits". (A nuclear energy liability policy is a policy issued by Mutual Atomic Energy Liability Underwriters, Nuclear Energy Liability Insurance Association, or Nuclear Insurance Association of Canada or their successors.)" This is exclusion 20. MSO's exclusion (12.) is similar, as is ISO's exclusion 20.

Workers Compensation

An exclusion common to MSO, ISO, and AAIS applies to workers compensation. ISO precludes coverage for:

19. "Bodily injury" to any person eligible to receive any benefits:

    a. Voluntarily provided; or

    b. Required to be provided;

    by an "insured" under any:

    (1) Workers' compensation law;

    (2) Nonoccupational disability law; or

    (3) Occupational disease law.

Remember, homeowners forms do not cover this exposure either. The exclusion in the ISO homeowners forms is identical to that in the umbrella, above.

The same is true of the MSO homeowners form and umbrella form, where the exclusion is:

17. Workers Compensation and Similar Laws Exclusion: We do not cover *bodily injury* to anyone eligible to receive benefits under a disability, occupational disease, workers' compensation, or similar law when benefits are required to be provided or are voluntarily made available by any *insured*.

Likewise, the AAIS umbrella form mirrors the homeowners, in that there is no coverage for:

22. "bodily injury" to a person, including a "domestic employee", if:

    a. the "insured" has a workers' compensation policy covering the injury" or

    b. benefits are payable or are required to be provided by an "insured" because of the existence, application, or enforcement of any provisions of any workers' compensation, non-occupational disability, occupational disease, or like law.

AAIS has an additional exclusion, not found in the ISO or MSO forms, and that is for:

39. "sickness, disease, or death of a "domestic employee" unless a written notice is received by "us" within 36 months after the end of the policy period in which the injury occurred."

Remember that there is coverage for bodily injury to a domestic employee with regard to "aircraft liability" arising out of duties in the course of employment, so naturally the insurer would want to be made aware as soon as possible of a potential suit. (See Chapter 5, "Recreational Motor Vehicles and Other Fun Stuff".)

Uncommon Exclusions

We conclude the discussion of exclusions with some that are not in each of the MSO, ISO, and AAIS umbrella forms.

Punitive Damages

MSO, in exclusion 8.c., declares "We do not cover any exemplary or punitive damages." The other forms are silent.

Loss Assessment

As might be expected, neither the American Association of Insurance Services (AAIS) nor the Insurance Services Office (ISO) personal umbrella forms provide coverage, since both provide coverage in the homeowners. (The basic amounts are ISO, $1,000; AAIS, $1,500. These may be increased.) The AAIS form, in exclusion 35., states that it will not provide liability coverage for "any assessment levied by a homeowners, condominium, mobile-homeowners, or similar residential association." ISO, in exclusion B., says "Liability coverage does not apply to any assessment charged against you as a member of an association, corporation or community of property owners." The MSO form is silent.

Contractual Liability

The AAIS, MSO, and ISO homeowners forms provide contractual liability—that is, liability assumed by an insured—to some extent. The ISO forms state:

Coverage E – Personal Liability, does not apply to:

1. Liability:

   a. Under any contract or agreement entered into by an insured. However, this exclusion does not apply to written contracts:

      (1) That directly relate to the ownership, maintenance or use of an "insured location"; or

      (2) Where the liability of others is assumed by the insured prior to an occurrence;

> unless excluded in a. above [loss assessment, which is provided elsewhere as an additional coverage] or elsewhere in this policy…

The AAIS forms agree:

3. Contracts

   a. We pay for damages for "bodily injury" or "property damage":

      1) for which an "insured" is liable under a written contract that directly relates to the ownership, maintenance, or use of an "insured premises"; or

      2) for which "you" are liable under a written contract, made before the loss, in which you have assumed the liability of others.

The loss causing the "bodily injury" or "property damage" must have occurred during the policy period.

The MSO form, like the AAIS and ISO forms, grants coverage for "your liability to pay damages, otherwise covered by this policy, in connection with written contracts made prior to the occurrence from which liability arises for: A. Liability of others assumed by *you*. B. Maintenance, ownership, or use of an *insured premises*." The MSO coverage continues that the insurer will not cover "any liability for loss assessments; or damage caused by explosion, fire or smoke." (But remember that there is coverage for an insured for property in his or her care caused by explosion, fire or smoke.)

Interestingly, the AAIS form is the only umbrella form of the three to specifically address contractual liability, which it does in exclusion 34. There is no coverage for liability under a contract or an agreement entered into by an insured; however, the exclusion does not apply to the extent that "such liability is covered by 'underlying insurance' at the time of the 'occurrence' or offense or would have been covered but for the exhaustion of its 'limits'."

Although it might appear strange that contractual liability is not addressed, remember that if a covered liability claim involving contractual liability is made under the homeowners, the umbrella will respond.

One Uniquely MSO

The MSO form contains one exclusion not found in AAIS or ISO: "We do not cover any fine, pecuniary, or forfeiture to any federal, state or local governmental unit."

And Finally...

Both AAIS and ISO have several exclusions that may be used to tailor an umbrella to meet specific circumstances. For example, a driver with an abysmal driving record may be excluded, as with ISO DL 98 23; a biting canine (Bowser, not tooth) may find his owner has no coverage for his actions. (In the MSO form Phydeaux's coverage restriction is found in the Ohio amendatory endorsement.) Consult the manuals for information.

Chapter 8

Conditions and Provisions

Introduction

As might be expected, umbrella forms contain conditions. Although the conditions of the AAIS, MSO, and ISO forms are similar, they are not necessarily identical. We will take a look at them, but having said that, probably the most important is the maintenance of underlying insurance. Umbrellas do not drop down to cover a gap triggered by the insured's inability to keep coverage.

Maintenance of Underlying Insurance; Retained Limit

Although maintenance of underlying insurance was discussed in the first chapter, and mentioned again above, the importance of this condition cannot be overemphasized. If the insured allows a policy to lapse—say, forgets to pay the homeowners insurance premium—the umbrella policy will not drop down to provide coverage if there is a loss. If the insured is responsible for carrying underlying limits of $300,000 comprehensive personal liability, the umbrella will respond as if these limits were in place. If the usual retained limit is $250, following the lapse it will be $300,250.

The minimum required limits for the programs are:

AAIS:

> Auto: 250/500/100 or 500 CSL (other, such as a motor home, refer to company)
>
> Personal liability: 300,000
>
> Watercraft, unlicensed recreational motor vehicle: 300,000 CSL
>
> The deductible is $1,000 for losses not covered by underlying insurance.

ISO:

> Auto: 250/500/100
>
> Personal liability: 300,000

The deductible is $250 for losses not covered by underlying insurance.

MSO:

Auto: 500/500/100 or 500 CSL for households with youthful drivers with one moving violation, otherwise 300/300/100 or 250/500/100 or 300CSL

Personal liability: 300,000 CSL

Unlicensed recreational vehicles, watercraft: 300,000 CSL

The deductible is $250.

With regard to maintenance of underlying insurance, the ISO form declares that "You must maintain the 'underlying insurance' at the full limits stated in the Declarations and with no change to more restrictive conditions during the term of this Policy. If any 'underlying insurance' is canceled or not renewed and not replaced, you must notify us at once. If you fail to maintain 'underlying insurance', we will not be liable under this Policy for more than we would have been liable if that 'underlying insurance' was in effect."

The AAIS form also declares that the insured must maintain "underlying limits" in full force during the policy period, and then adds "If any 'underlying insurance' is canceled or not renewed and not replaced or is at any time materially changed in 'limits' or coverages, 'you' must notify 'us' within thirty days of the effective date of such cancellation, nonrenewal, or change. 'We' will not be liable under this policy for more than 'we' would have been liable if that 'underlying insurance' had not been terminated or had been kept at its original 'limits' or coverages." The AAIS form adds that a reduction or exhaustion of any aggregate limit (note, this refers to an aggregate limit, which is possible under the AAIS program) in underlying insurance because of payments for judgments will not be considered failure to keep underlying insurance in full force.

Finally, the MSO form advises that "the insurance afforded by each policy listed in the Schedule of Underlying Insurance in the Umbrella Declarations will be maintained for the full term of this insurance." Then, like the AAIS form, the MSO form states that the provision does not apply to the reduction of aggregate limits because of the payment of claims. However, the insured must renew any such policies at the required amount of coverage. Should the insured not comply, the insurer will pay a covered loss only to the extent it would have been paid had the insured complied with the requirement. The insured must give the insurer notice of any change in underlying coverage, such as a termination, limits, exhaustion of aggregate limits, etc.

With regard to the retained limit, the AAIS form, in the section Excess Insurance (1.), states that if there is no underlying insurance (other than the required underlying insurance, or insurance from a bankrupt insurer) then the umbrella applies as excess over the retained limit shown on the declarations. The AAIS manual gives $1,000 as a base retained limit for occurrences not covered by underlying insurance.

The ISO form defines a retained limit, but includes within the definition a deductible:

O. "Retained limit" means:

1. The total limits of any "underlying insurance" and any other insurance that applies to an "occurrence or offense" which:

   a. Are available to an "insured"; or

   b. Would have been available except for the bankruptcy or insolvency of an insurer providing "underlying insurance"' or

2. The deductible, if any, as stated in the Declarations, if the "occurrence" or offense:

   a. Is covered by this Policy, and

   b. Is not covered by "underlying insurance" or any other insurance.

Finally, we quote the MSO conditions in some length since they give a good summary of how umbrellas work with regard to payment:

B. If the *occurrence* is covered by *underlying primary insurance*, *our* limit of liability under this insurance applies to any damages which exceed the limits of liability of all the underlying primary insurance policies together with any other collectible insurance available to the insured.

C. If the occurrence is not covered by underlying primary insurance, but is covered by this insurance, then our limit of liability applies to damages which exceed the Self-Insured Retention limit shown in the Umbrella Declarations. The insured shall retain this amount as self insurance.

However, this condition does not apply when the following Paragraph D. applies.

D. When coverage and payment that might otherwise have been available to the *insured* under *underlying primary insurance* (with respect to any covered *occurrence*) is not available because such *underlying primary insurance*:

1. Has been terminated, reduced in coverage, or reduced in limits (other than a reduction of aggregate limits because of claim payments); or

2. Is not payable because the *underlying insurer* is bankrupt, insolvent, or is otherwise generally relieved of making payments by judicial decree, legislation or regulation; or

3. Is not payable because the *insured* failed to comply with contractual requirements of such; then

We will pay solely as though the applicable *underlying primary insurance* is fully payable.

For example: if the otherwise covered damages are $500,000 and the subject primary policy would have provided $300,000 in payment, then *we* will pay no more than $200,000 ($500,000 less $300,000).

In such cases, *we* are not obligated to provide the defense and supplementary payments described in Section I.B. although *we* retain the right to do so.

Bankruptcy of Underlying Insurer

We mentioned the insolvency of an underlying insurer in the paragraphs above. Unfortunately, if the insured's underlying insurer becomes insolvent, the umbrella insurance will not drop down to fill this coverage gap. Rather, it will respond as if the underlying coverage was in place. The forms all have this provision: in the MSO form, it is D.2. (above); in the AAIS, it is 3. under "How Much We Pay," and in the ISO form, it is C. in the "General Provisions" section.

Make sure that any insureds with personal umbrellas are placed with top-rated carriers. If you suspect a particular insurer may have financial difficulties, promptly move the business from that carrier. If an insured arrives at your office with a quote from "Fly-by-Nite" insurance company, with a request to just check out the coverage with rock-bottom prices, don't jump on this particular bandwagon.

Notification to Insurer

The insured is responsible for notifying the umbrella insurer of any changes to underlying policies. This includes, for example, notification of any additional motor vehicles (the base premium for most umbrella forms is predicated on one home and one or two cars,), or a newly acquired watercraft that might require a separate policy. If the terms of an underlying policy are amended so that coverage becomes restricted in some manner—for example, a driver is excluded because of a poor driving record—the insurer must be notified. Failure to notify an insurer of changes can jeopardize coverage. In the ISO form, this condition is included in condition IV., Maintenance of Underlying Insurance; in the AAIS form, it is 7. Maintenance of Underlying Insurance, and in the MSO form, it is 10. Maintenance of Underlying Insurance. The MSO form also advises that the insurer will not cover "*bodily injury, property damage* or *personal injury* arising out of newly acquired *aircraft, motor vehicles* or *watercraft* unless *we a*re notified within 30 days of such acquisition."

Duties after a Loss

Following a loss, there are duties the named insured is required to fulfill. We will give only the ISO form's loss conditions, because both AAIS (What Must be Done in Case of Loss, 1 to 8) and MSO (Duties of Insureds, 8.) are similar. One important thing to remember is that failure to comply with these conditions may void any coverage otherwise available. In condition V., Duties After Loss, the ISO form declares:

In case of an "occurrence" or offense likely to involve the insurance under this Policy, you or another "insured" will perform the following duties that apply. We have no duty to provide coverage under this Policy if your failure to comply with the following duties is prejudicial to us. You will help us by seeing that these duties are performed:

A. Give written notice to us or our agent as soon as is practical. Such notice shall set forth:

   1. The identity of the Policy and named insured shown in the Declarations;

   2. Reasonably available information about the time, place and circumstances of the "occurrence" or offense; and

   3. The names and addresses of any claimants and witnesses.

B. If a claim is made or a suit is brought against an "insured", the "insured" must:

   1. Notify us immediately in writing;

   2. Cooperate with us in the investigation, settlement or defense of any claim or suit;

3. Promptly forward to us every notice, demand, summons or other process relating to the "occurrence" or offense;

4. At our request, help us:

   a. To make settlement;

   b. To enforce any right of contribution or indemnity against any person or organization who may be liable to an "insured"

   c. With the conduct of suits and attend hearings and trials; and

   d. To secure and give evidence and obtain the attendance of witnesses.

C. The "insured" will not, except at the "insured's" own cost, voluntarily make payment, assume obligation or incur expense to others.

Many people think that, in event of an at-fault accident that does not seem too severe, some money given to the "victim" will make the problem disappear. Or, the "victim" might take the insured's information, and tell him or her that there's no problem—that is, until later when the "no problem" turns into a several thousand dollar claim for vehicle damage, bodily injury, etc. The latter condition (C.) in this list should be emphasized to insureds.

Defense and Additional Coverages

Frequently appearing as part of the insuring agreement, but sometimes as a separate condition, is the insurer's duty to defend. The umbrella insurer has no duty to defend a suit, though, if the underlying insurance applies and the underlying insurer will provide a defense. Obviously, if no underlying policy applies to an occurrence covered by the umbrella, the umbrella insurer will assume the primary defense for a covered claim. The umbrella insurer has the right to join in defense with the underlying insurer if it appears that a suit is likely to involve the umbrella coverage. The MSO(I.B.), ISO (II.B), and AAIS Defense Coverages are similar, and so we will look at the AAIS:

1. "We" have the right to defend, investigate, and settle any claim or "suit" seeking damages covered by this policy. "We" may elect at any time to participate with an "insured" and with any "underlying insurer" or other insurer in the defense, investigation, and settlement of any claim or "suit" arising out of an "occurrence" or an offense that, in "our" opinion, may involve damages to which this policy may apply. Any such defense will be provided at "our" expense by counsel that "we" choose.

However, "we" have no obligation to share in or contribute to any costs or expenses incurred by any "underlying insurer" or other insurer.

2. "We" have the duty to defend any claim or "suit" seeking damages to which this insurance applies, but only with respect to damages:

   a. covered by "underlying insurance" or any other valid and collectible insurance available to the "insured" except for exhaustion of a "limit" of such "underlying insurance" or other insurance by the payment of losses; or

   b. not covered by "underlying insurance" or any other valid and collectible insurance available to the "insured".

   However, "we" have no duty to defend a claim or "suit" seeking damages for an amount that does not exceed the Personal Umbrella Liability Coverage Retained Limit shown on the "declarations".

   Such defense will be provided at "our" expense by counsel that "we" choose.

   "Our" duty to defend ends when "we" have paid an amount equal to the "limit" that applies as a result of a judgment or written settlement.

   If "we" are prevented by law or otherwise prevented from carrying out this agreement, "we" will pay the "insured" for any expense incurred with "our" written consent.

This latter provision does not appear in either the MSO or the ISO forms; however, the intent is the same in all. The provision is stating that if, for example, an insured is faced with a lawsuit brought in Italy the insurer will pay for the insured's defense, even if a U.S. attorney cannot be used. The other forms simply state that the insurer will provide a defense "at our expense."

In the AAIS form, the defense coverage continues with what are, in the ISO form, additional coverages (II.C.). The MSO form also lists these under the section "Defense of Claims or Suits." These spell out the monies that the insurer is prepared to lay out for costs incurred by the insurer and the insured in a suit the insurer defends, premiums on any required bond (although the insurer need not apply for or furnish the bonds), up to $250 per day for loss of earnings, but not loss of other income, for time spent away from work by the insured at the insurer's request, interest on a judgment, and prejudgment interest on the part of a judgment paid by the insurer. However, if the insurer offers to pay the policy limit, then no prejudgment interest will be paid on the period of time after the offer.

Bankruptcy of the Insured

One provision that appears in the three umbrella forms, and, indeed, in many other forms, is the one promising that an insured's insolvency or bankruptcy will not relieve the insurer of any obligation under the policy. In the ISO form, this is provision B., in the MSO, it is 3., and in the AAIS, it is condition 2.

Conformity with State Law

As is common with insurance forms, any terms in them that conflict with state or local laws are amended to conform with the state or local law. The AAIS form states, in Condition 3., that: "Terms" in conflict with the laws of the state in which "your" mailing address shown on the "declarations" is located are changed to conform to such laws." The MSO form hedges its bets by stating, in condition 7., that "It is agreed by *us* that the provisions in this coverage form are amended to conform to all applicable statutory requirements." Oddly, the ISO umbrella form does not have this provision, although ISO homeowners and PAP forms do. It might be that, since ISO operates in virtually all states (and territories), it can apply an amendatory endorsement detailing any state changes.

Suit or Action against the Insurer

This provision is commonly found in the policies, and it is that the insured may not bring suit against the insurer until all policy provisions have been complied with. Also, the umbrella forms also state that umbrella insurers cannot be brought into a suit against their own insureds. In the AAIS form, this is condition 6., in the MSO, it is condition 1., and in the ISO form, it is provision J.

Cancellation

Umbrella forms are infrequently regulated by the states, and so cancellation may be for any reason (New York is one exception, since all personal lines of insurance are regulated.) The cancellation provisions are: ISO, provision K., and the MSO, condition 4. The AAIS form does not contain a cancellation provision; however, it is found on endorsement PU 0605, attached to the policy.

Concealment or Fraud

Given the amount of coverage at stake—never less than a million dollars—it would seem that a provision stating that the policy could be voided if the insurer learned of any intentional concealment or misrepresentation of any material fact or circumstances, or any fraudulent conduct relating to the insurance, would be included in every umbrella form. This is not the case, however. Of the three forms, MSO is the only one to declare that "This coverage form is void if, either before or after an *occurrence* or claim, any *insured* misrepresents or knowingly conceals any material fact or circumstance, commits fraud, or swears falsely relating to any aspect of this insurance (including the information *we* relied upon in issuing this contract). However, if *we* specifically choose not to declare this coverage form void, we do not provide insurance here to, or for the benefit of, any such *insureds*." This is saying that the insurer has the right to declare that the policy is void—that is, that coverage has never existed—but it may choose not to do so. In that event, there will be no insurance coverage for any insured who has committed the fraud. Both the ISO and AAIS forms, in conditions D. and 8. respectively, state that no coverage will be provided for the insured who has committed the fraud.

Modification of Policy Terms

All of the forms contain provisions to the effect that only the insurer may modify policy terms. In the MSO form, this is condition 5., in the AAIS form, it is 3., and in the ISO form, it is condition M.

Severability of Insurance

One would also expect the severability of insurance clause to appear in every umbrella form, and it does. Remember, though, that when "an insured" is used in the umbrella form the term refers to "one or more insureds." Therefore, as in underlying policies, when an insured is charged with committing an intentional act resulting in bodily injury, for example, there will be no coverage for other insureds with regard to the same act. In the AAIS form, this is provision 4., in the ISO, I., and in the MSO form, condition 13.

Appeals

The three umbrella forms all declare that if the insured's underlying insurer decides not to appeal a judgment that exceeds the required underlying limit, then the umbrella insurer has the right to do so. In that event, the insurer will pay all costs, taxes, expenses, and interest earned. Doing so will not reduce the umbrella limit of liability. These are provisions A., D., and 1. in the ISO, MSO, and AAIS forms respectively.

Finally….

Here are some miscellaneous provisions that are unique to a particular form. AAIS's provision 9. states the policy period will be found on the

Declarations page. Provision 5. allows the insurer to inspect the insured's property, and 10. is a subrogation clause. In the ISO form, provision H. gives the policy period and territory (anywhere in the world), and G. is a subrogation clause. We conclude with the MSO provision F., which states "Any collected recovery or salvage will be deducted from such excess liability."

Appendix A

Personal Liability Checklist

Date:

Named Insured:

Address:

City/State/Zip:

Phone: Business__________________

Home______________________

Cell________________________

X-date:

Premises Liability:

	Yes	**No**
Are there any domestic or residence employees?	☐	☐
If yes, is workers compensation required?	☐	☐
Any business activities on residence premises?	☐	☐
Describe:__________________________		
Special coverage necessary?	☐	☐
Is there an in-home business?	☐	☐
Is there on-premises day care?	☐	☐
Is professional liability coverage required?	☐	☐
Is any portion of any residence premises rented to others?	☐	☐
if so, usage:_________________________		
Are there any unusual pets?	☐	☐

Farming:

	Yes	No
Does insured engage in farming operations? (if yes, specify type)	☐	☐
incidental	☐	☐
custom farming	☐	☐
farm employees	☐	☐
livestock	☐	☐

Motorized Recreational Vehicles:

Does insured own a snowmobile?	☐	☐
Does insured own an amphibious vehicle?	☐	☐
Does insured own an ATV?	☐	☐
Does insured own a go-kart?	☐	☐
Does insured own a dune buggy?	☐	☐
Does insured own a golf cart?	☐	☐
If yes to any, where used?________________________		
Do any need to be licensed?	☐	☐

Watercraft:

Does insured own a boat/yacht?	☐	☐
sailboat length:________		
powerboat length:________		
inboard or inboard/outdrive?		
horsepower:_______		
Any watercraft with a crew?		
Is it used for water skiing?	☐	☐
Is it rented to others?	☐	☐
Any jet skis, wet bikes, or the like?	☐	☐
Principal operator(s)/ages:____________________		

Aircraft:

Does the insured own any aircraft?	☐	☐
How titled:____________________		
How used:____________________		
Is it rented to others?	☐	☐

Rental Residential Property:

	Yes	No
Does the insured have rental (residential) property?	☐	☐
number of families ____________		
Is there any business conducted on premises?	☐	☐
if so, what?		

Miscellaneous:

Are there any foster children cared for?	☐	☐
Are there any business activities on premises?	☐	☐
if yes, describe:____________________		
Does insured volunteer for a non-profit org.?	☐	☐
Does the insured have paid civic/public duties?	☐	☐
Is insured a corporate director?	☐	☐
Do insured/insured's children do any babysitting on premises?	☐	☐
Is there a swimming pool on premises?	☐	☐
if so, is it fenced?		
Any other "attractive nuisances" such as a trampoline?	☐	☐
if so, describe_________________		

Personal Automobiles:

List all personal vehicles (include vans and pickups); who drives them; where insured; limits of liability coverage on each; any policy restrictions changing coverage from standard.

Do insured family members use insured's auto?	☐	☐
Does insured own any pickups or vans?	☐	☐
Does insured own any trailers?	☐	☐
Does insured have any leased autos?	☐	☐
Does insured regularly use nonowned autos?		
Is the insured furnished a company car?	☐	☐
Does insured use personal vehicle as a public/livery conveyance?	☐	☐
Is insured's vehicle driven by domestic employee(s)?	☐	☐
Is insured's vehicle used for any business purposes?	☐	☐
Is there any other applicable insurance?	☐	☐
Are there any miscellaneous type vehicles (e.g. motorcycles, motorhomes)?	☐	☐

Special Considerations

	Yes	No
Does insured need uninsured/underinsured motorist coverage?	☐	☐
Does the insured have any youthful drivers?	☐	☐
Does insured use auto(s) outside U.S.?	☐	☐

General Comments:

Forms

PERSONAL LIABILITY
DL 98 01 02 15

PERSONAL UMBRELLA LIABILITY POLICY

AGREEMENT

In return for payment of the premium and subject to all the terms of this Policy, we agree with you as follows:

I. Definitions

A. Throughout this Policy, "you" and "your" refer to:

1. The "named insured" shown in the Declarations; and

2. The spouse if a resident of the same household.

B. "We", "us" and "our" refer to the company providing this insurance.

C. For purposes of this Policy, a private passenger type auto, pickup or van shall be deemed to be owned by a person if leased:

1. Under a written agreement to that person; and

2. For a continuous period of at least six months.

Other words and phrases are defined. They are in quotation marks when used.

D. "Aircraft Liability", "Hovercraft Liability", "Recreational Motor Vehicle Liability" and "Watercraft Liability", subject to the provisions in **2.** below, mean the following:

1. Liability for "bodily injury" or "property damage" arising out of:

a. The ownership of such vehicle or craft by an "insured";

b. The maintenance, occupancy, operation, use, loading or unloading of such vehicle or craft by any person;

c. The entrustment of such vehicle or craft by an "insured" to any person;

d. The failure to supervise or negligent supervision of any person involving such vehicle or craft by an "insured"; or

e. Vicarious liability, whether or not imposed by law, for the actions of a child or minor involving such vehicle or craft.

2. For the purpose of this definition:

a. Aircraft means any contrivance used or designed for flight, except model or hobby aircraft not used or designed to carry people or cargo;

b. Hovercraft means a self-propelled motorized ground-effect vehicle and includes, but is not limited to, flarecraft and air cushion vehicles;

c. Watercraft means a craft principally designed to be propelled on or in water by wind, engine power or electric motor; and

d. Recreational Motor Vehicle means a "recreational motor vehicle" as defined in Paragraph **N.**

E. "Auto" means:

1. A private passenger motor vehicle, motorcycle, moped or motor home;

2. A vehicle designed to be pulled by a private passenger motor vehicle or motor home; or

3. A farm wagon or farm implement while towed by a private passenger motor vehicle or motor home.

F. "Bodily injury" means bodily harm, sickness or disease, including required care, loss of services and death that results.

G. "Business" means:

1. A trade, profession or occupation engaged in on a full-time, part-time or occasional basis; or

2. Any other activity engaged in for money or other compensation, except the following:

a. One or more activities, not described in **b.** through **d.** below, for which no "insured" receives more than $2,000 in total compensation for the 12 months before the beginning of the policy period;

b. Volunteer activities for which no money is received other than payment for expenses incurred to perform the activity;

c. Providing home day care services for which no compensation is received, other than the mutual exchange of such services; or

d. The rendering of home day care services to a relative of an "insured".

H. "Family member" means a resident of your household who is:

1. Your relative, including a ward or foster child; or

2. Under the age of 21 and in the care of you or an "insured" who is age 21 or over.

I. "Fuel system" means:

1. One or more containers, tanks or vessels which have a total combined storage capacity of 100 or more U.S. gallons of liquid fuel; and:

a. Are, or were, located on any single location covered by "underlying insurance"; and

b. Are, or were, used to hold liquid fuel that is intended to be used solely for one or more of the following:

(1) To heat or cool a building;

(2) To heat water;

(3) To cook food; or

(4) To power motor vehicles, other motorized land conveyances or watercraft owned by an "insured";

2. Any pumping apparatus, which includes the motor, gauge, nozzle, hose or pipes that are, or were, connected to one or more containers, tanks or vessels described in Paragraph **I.1.;**

3. Filler pipes and flues connected to one or more containers, tanks or vessels described in Paragraph **I.1.;**

4. A boiler, furnace or a water heater, the liquid fuel for which is stored in a container, tank or vessel described in Paragraph **I.1.;**

5. Fittings and pipes connecting the boiler, furnace or water heater to one or more containers, tanks or vessels described in Paragraph **I.1.;** or

6. A structure that is specifically designed and built to hold the liquid fuel that escapes from one or more containers, tanks or vessels described in Paragraph **I.1.**

J. "Insured" means:

1. You.

2. A "family member".

3. Any person using an "auto", "recreational motor vehicle", or watercraft, which is owned by you and covered under this Policy. Any person using a temporary substitute for such "auto" or "recreational motor vehicle" is also an "insured".

4. Any other person or organization but only with respect to the legal responsibility for acts or omissions of you or any "family member" while you or any "family member" is using an "auto" or "recreational motor vehicle" covered under this Policy. However, the owner or lessor of an "auto" or "recreational motor vehicle" loaned to or hired for use by an "insured" or on an "insured's" behalf, is not an "insured".

5. With respect to animals owned by you or any "family member", any person or organization legally responsible for such animals. However, a person or organization using or having custody of such animals in the course of any "business" or without the consent of the owner is not an "insured".

K. "Occurrence" means an accident, including continuous or repeated exposure to substantially the same general harmful conditions, which results, during the policy period, in:

1. "Bodily injury"; or

2. "Property damage".

L. "Personal injury" means injury arising out of one or more of the following offenses, but only if the offense was committed during the policy period:

1. False arrest, detention or imprisonment;

2. Malicious prosecution;

3. The wrongful eviction from, wrongful entry into, or invasion of the right of private occupancy of a room, dwelling or premises that a person occupies, committed by or on behalf of its owner, landlord or lessor;

4. Oral or written publication, in any manner, of material that slanders or libels a person or organization or disparages a person's or organization's goods, products or services; or

5. Oral or written publication, in any manner, of material that violates a person's right of privacy.

M. "Property damage" means physical injury to, destruction of, or loss of use of tangible property.

N. "Recreational motor vehicle" means:

1. All-terrain vehicle;

2. Dune buggy;

3. Golf cart;

4. Snowmobile; or

5. Any other motorized land vehicle which is designed for recreational use off public roads.

O. "Retained limit" means:

1. The total limits of any "underlying insurance" and any other insurance that applies to an "occurrence" or offense which:

a. Are available to an "insured"; or

b. Would have been available except for the bankruptcy or insolvency of an insurer providing "underlying insurance"; or

2. The deductible, if any, as stated in the Declarations, if the "occurrence" or offense:

a. Is covered by this Policy; and

b. Is not covered by "underlying insurance" or any other insurance.

P. "Underlying insurance" means any policy providing the "insured" with primary liability insurance covering one or more of the types of liability listed in the Declarations and at limits no less than the retained policy limits shown for those types of liability listed in the Declarations.

II. Coverages

A. Insuring Agreement

We will pay damages, in excess of the "retained limit", for:

1. "Bodily injury" or "property damage" for which an "insured" becomes legally liable due to an "occurrence" to which this insurance applies; and

2. "Personal injury" for which an "insured" becomes legally liable due to one or more offenses listed under the definition of "personal injury" to which this insurance applies.

Damages include prejudgment interest awarded against an "insured".

B. Defense Coverage

1. If a claim is made or a suit is brought against an "insured" for damages because of "bodily injury" or "property damage" caused by an "occurrence" or "personal injury" caused by an offense to which this Policy applies, we:

a. Will provide a defense at our expense by counsel of our choice, even if the suit is groundless, false or fraudulent. However, we are not obligated to defend any suit or settle any claim if:

(1) The "occurrence" or offense is covered by other "underlying insurance" available to the "insured"; or

(2) There is no applicable "underlying insurance" in effect at the time of the "occurrence" or offense and the amount of damages claimed or incurred is less than the applicable deductible amount shown in the Declarations;

b. May join, at our expense, with the "insured" or any insurer providing "underlying insurance" in the investigation, defense or settlement of any claim or suit which we believe may require payment under this Policy.

However, we will not contribute to the costs and expenses incurred by any insurer providing "underlying insurance"; and

c. Will pay any expense incurred for the "insured's" defense, with our written consent, in any country where we are prevented from defending an "insured" because of laws or other reasons.

2. We may investigate and settle any claim or suit that we decide is appropriate. Our duty to settle or defend ends when our limit of liability for the "occurrence" or offense has been exhausted by payment of judgments or settlements.

C. Additional Coverages

We will pay:

1. Expenses we incur and costs taxed against an "insured" in any suit we defend;

2. Premiums on bonds required in a suit we defend, but not for bond amounts to the extent they exceed our limit of liability. We need not apply for or furnish any bond;
3. Reasonable expenses incurred by an "insured" at our request, including actual loss of earnings (but not loss of other income) up to $250 per day, for assisting us in the investigation or defense of a claim or suit; and
4. Interest on our share of the judgment which accrues after entry of the judgment and before we pay or tender, or deposit in court, that part of the judgment which does not exceed the limit of liability that applies.

These payments will not reduce the limit of liability.

D. Limit Of Liability

Our total liability under this Policy for all damages resulting from any one "occurrence" or offense will not be more than the Limit Of Liability as shown in the Declarations of this Policy. This limit is the most we will pay regardless of the number of "insureds", claims made, persons injured, or vehicles involved in an accident.

III. Exclusions

A. The coverages provided by this Policy do not apply to:

1. "Bodily injury" or "property damage" which is expected or intended by an "insured" even if the resulting "bodily injury" or "property damage":
   a. Is of a different kind, quality or degree than initially expected or intended; or
   b. Is sustained by a different person, entity or property than initially expected or intended.

   However, this exclusion **(A.1.)** does not apply to:
   (1) "Bodily injury" or "property damage" resulting from the use of reasonable force by an "insured" to protect persons or property; or
   (2) "Bodily injury" or "property damage" resulting from the use of reasonable force by an "insured" to prevent or eliminate danger in the operation of "autos", "recreational motor vehicles" or watercraft;
2. "Personal injury":
   a. Caused by or at the direction of an "insured" with the knowledge that the act would violate the rights of another and would inflict "personal injury";
   b. Arising out of oral or written publication of material, if done by or at the direction of an "insured" with knowledge of its falsity;
   c. Arising out of oral or written publication of material whose first publication took place before the beginning of the policy period;
   d. Arising out of a criminal act committed by or at the direction of an "insured"; or
   e. Sustained by any person as a result of an offense directly or indirectly related to the employment of this person by an "insured";
3. "Bodily injury", "personal injury" or "property damage" arising out of or in connection with a "business":
   a. Engaged in by an "insured"; or
   b. Conducted from:
      (1) Any part of a premises owned by or rented to an "insured"; or
      (2) Vacant land owned by or rented to an "insured".

   This exclusion **(A.3.)** applies but is not limited to an act or omission, regardless of its nature or circumstance, involving a service or duty rendered, promised, owed, or implied to be provided because of the nature of the "business".

   However, this exclusion **(A.3.)** does not apply to:
   (1) The rental or holding for rental of:
      (a) The residence premises shown in the Declarations:
         (i) On an occasional basis if used only as a residence;
         (ii) In part, for use only as a residence, unless a single-family unit is intended for use by the occupying family to lodge more than two roomers or boarders; or
         (iii) In part, as an office, school, studio or private garage;

(b) Any part of a one- to four-family dwelling, other than the residence premises, to the extent that personal liability coverage is provided by "underlying insurance";

(c) A condominium, cooperative, or apartment unit, other than the residence premises, to the extent that personal liability coverage is provided by "underlying insurance";

(2) Civic or public activities performed by an "insured" without compensation other than reimbursement of expenses;

(3) An insured minor involved in self-employed "business" pursuits, which are occasional or part-time and customarily undertaken on that basis by minors. A minor means a person who has not attained his or her:

(a) 18th birthday; or

(b) 21st birthday if a full-time student;

(4) The use of an "auto" you own, or a temporary substitute for such "auto", by you, a "family member" or a partner, agent or employee of you or a "family member" while employed or otherwise engaged in the "business" of:

(a) Selling;

(b) Repairing;

(c) Servicing;

(d) Storing; or

(e) Parking;

vehicles designed for use mainly on public highways;

(5) The use of an "auto" for "business" purposes, other than an auto business, by an "insured";

4. "Bodily injury" or "property damage" arising out of the ownership or operation of an "auto" while it is being used as a public or livery conveyance. This exclusion **(A.4.)** does not apply to:

a. A share-the-expense car pool; or

b. The ownership or operation of an "auto" while it is being used for volunteer or charitable purposes;

5. "Bodily injury" or "property damage" arising out of the ownership, maintenance or use of an "auto" while:

a. Enrolled in a personal vehicle sharing program under the terms of a written agreement; and

b. Being used in connection with such personal vehicle sharing program by anyone other than you or any "family member";

6. "Bodily injury", "personal injury" or "property damage" arising out of the rendering of or failure to render professional services;

7. "Aircraft Liability";

8. "Hovercraft Liability";

9. "Watercraft Liability".

However, this exclusion **(A.9.)** does not apply to the extent that watercraft coverage is provided by "underlying insurance" at the time of the "occurrence";

10. "Recreational Motor Vehicle Liability".

However, this exclusion **(A.10.)** does not apply with respect to any "recreational motor vehicle":

a. Owned by you or a "family member" to the extent that "recreational motor vehicle" coverage is provided by "underlying insurance" at the time of the "occurrence"; or

b. That you or a "family member" does not own;

11. "Bodily injury" or "property damage" caused directly or indirectly by war, including the following and any consequence of any of the following:

a. Undeclared war, civil war, insurrection, rebellion or revolution;

b. Warlike act by a military force or military personnel; or

c. Destruction, seizure or use for a military purpose.

Discharge of a nuclear weapon will be deemed a warlike act even if accidental;

12. A person using an "auto", "recreational motor vehicle" or watercraft without a reasonable belief that that person is entitled to do so. This exclusion **(A.12.)** does not apply to a "family member" using an "auto", "recreational motor vehicle" or watercraft you own;

13. The ownership, maintenance or use of:

a. Any "auto" for the purpose of:

(1) Participating or competing in; or

(2) Practicing or preparing for;

any prearranged or organized:

(a) Racing or speed contest; or

(b) Driver skill training or driver skill event; and

b. Any watercraft which, at the time of the "occurrence", is:

(1) Being operated in; or

(2) Practicing or preparing for;

any prearranged or organized:

(a) Race;

(b) Stunt activity;

(c) Speed contest; or

(d) Other competition.

However, this exclusion **(A.13.)** does not apply to:

(1) Motorcycle rider skill training in connection with a course designed by the Motorcycle Safety Foundation, or any similar course administered by any state agency, to improve motorcycle rider skills;

(2) A sailing vessel; or

(3) Watercraft involved in predicted log cruises;

14. "Bodily injury" or "personal injury" to you or a "family member".

This exclusion also applies to any claim made or suit brought:

a. To repay; or

b. Share damages with;

another person who may be obligated to pay damages because of "bodily injury" or "personal injury" to you or a "family member";

15. "Bodily injury" or "personal injury" arising out of:

a. The transmission of a communicable disease by an "insured";

b. Sexual molestation, corporal punishment or physical or mental abuse; or

c. The use, sale, manufacture, delivery, transfer or possession by any person of a Controlled Substance(s) as defined by the Federal Food and Drug Law at 21 U.S.C.A. Sections 811 and 812. Controlled Substances include but are not limited to cocaine, LSD, marijuana and all narcotic drugs. However, this exclusion **(A.15.)** does not apply to the legitimate use of prescription drugs by a person following the lawful orders of a licensed health care professional;

16. "Bodily injury", "personal injury" or "property damage" arising out of an act or omission of an "insured" as an officer or member of a board of directors of a corporation or organization. However, this exclusion **(A.16.)** does not apply if the corporation or organization is not-for-profit and the "insured" receives no compensation other than reimbursement of expenses;

17. "Property damage" to property owned by an "insured". This includes costs or expenses incurred by an "insured" or others to repair, replace, enhance, restore or maintain such property to prevent injury to a person or damage to property of others, whether on or away from the residence premises shown in the Declarations;

18. "Property damage" to property rented to, occupied or used by, or in the care, custody or control of, an "insured" to the extent that the "insured" is obligated by contract to provide insurance for such property. However, this exclusion **(A.18.)** does not apply to "property damage" caused by fire, smoke or explosion;

19. "Bodily injury" to any person eligible to receive any benefits:

a. Voluntarily provided; or

b. Required to be provided;

by an "insured" under any:

(1) Workers' compensation law;

(2) Nonoccupational disability law; or

(3) Occupational disease law;

20. "Bodily injury" or "property damage" for which an "insured" under this Policy:

a. Is also an insured under a nuclear energy liability policy issued by the:

(1) Nuclear Energy Liability Insurance Association;

(2) Mutual Atomic Energy Liability Underwriters; or

(3) Nuclear Insurance Association of Canada;

or any of their successors; or

b. Would be an insured under that policy but for the exhaustion of its limit of liability;

21. "Bodily injury", "personal injury" or "property damage" caused by an "occurrence" or offense involving the escape of fuel from a "fuel system";

22. "Bodily injury" or "personal injury" caused by an "occurrence" or offense involving the absorption, ingestion or inhalation of lead; or

23. "Personal injury" or "property damage" caused by an "occurrence" or offense of lead contamination.

B. Liability coverage does not apply to any assessment charged against you as a member of an association, corporation or community of property owners.

C. We do not provide:

1. Automobile no-fault or any similar coverage under this Policy; or

2. Uninsured Motorists Coverage, Underinsured Motorists Coverage, or any similar coverage unless this Policy is endorsed to provide such coverage.

IV. Maintenance Of Underlying Insurance

You must maintain the "underlying insurance" at the full limits stated in the Declarations and with no change to more restrictive conditions during the term of this Policy. If any "underlying insurance" is canceled or not renewed and not replaced, you must notify us at once.

If you fail to maintain "underlying insurance", we will not be liable under this Policy for more than we would have been liable if that "underlying insurance" was in effect.

V. Duties After Loss

In case of an "occurrence" or offense likely to involve the insurance under this Policy, you or another "insured" will perform the following duties that apply. We have no duty to provide coverage under this Policy if your failure to comply with the following duties is prejudicial to us. You will help us by seeing that these duties are performed:

A. Give written notice to us or our agent as soon as is practical. Such notice shall set forth:

1. The identity of the Policy and named insured shown in the Declarations;

2. Reasonably available information about the time, place and circumstances of the "occurrence" or offense; and

3. The names and addresses of any claimants and witnesses.

B. If a claim is made or a suit is brought against an "insured", the "insured" must:

1. Notify us immediately in writing;

2. Cooperate with us in the investigation, settlement or defense of any claim or suit;

3. Promptly forward to us every notice, demand, summons or other process relating to the "occurrence" or offense;

4. At our request, help us:

a. To make settlement;

b. To enforce any right of contribution or indemnity against any person or organization who may be liable to an "insured";

c. With the conduct of suits and attend hearings and trials; and

d. To secure and give evidence and obtain the attendance of witnesses.

C. The "insured" will not, except at the "insured's" own cost, voluntarily make payment, assume obligation or incur expense to others.

VI. General Provisions

A. Appeals

If an "insured" or any insurer providing "underlying insurance" elects not to appeal a judgment which exceeds the "retained limit", we may do so at our own expense. We will pay all costs, taxes, expenses and interest related to our appeal. These payments will not reduce the limit of liability.

B. Bankruptcy Of An Insured

Bankruptcy or insolvency of an "insured" will neither:

1. Relieve us of our obligations under this Policy; nor

2. Operate to cause this Policy to become primary in the event the "insured" is unable to satisfy the "retained limit" either because of insufficient "underlying insurance" or insufficient personal assets.

C. Bankruptcy Of An Underlying Insurer

In the event of bankruptcy or insolvency of any underlying insurer, the insurance afforded by this Policy shall not replace such "underlying insurance", but shall apply as if the "underlying insurance" was valid and collectible.

D. Fraud

We do not provide coverage for any "insured" who has made fraudulent statements or engaged in fraudulent conduct in connection with any "occurrence" or offense for which coverage is sought under this Policy.

E. Liberalization Clause

If we make a change which broadens coverage under this edition of our policy without additional premium charge, that change will automatically apply to your insurance as of the date we implement the change in your state, provided that this implementation date falls within 60 days prior to or during the policy period stated in the Declarations.

This Liberalization Clause does not apply to changes implemented with a general program revision that includes both broadenings and restrictions in coverage, whether that general program revision is implemented through introduction of:

1. A subsequent edition of this Policy; or
2. An amendatory endorsement.

F. Other Insurance

The coverage afforded by this Policy is excess over any other insurance available to an "insured", except insurance written specifically to be excess over this Policy.

G. Our Right To Recover Payment

If we make a payment under this Policy and the person to or for whom payment was made has a right to recover damages from another, we shall be subrogated to that right. That person shall do:

1. Whatever is necessary to enable us to exercise our rights; and
2. Nothing after loss to prejudice them.

H. Policy Period And Territory

The policy period is stated in the Declarations. This Policy applies to an "occurrence" or offense which takes place anywhere in the world.

I. Severability Of Insurance

This insurance applies separately to each "insured". However, this provision will not increase our limit of liability for any one "occurrence" or offense.

J. Suit Against Us

1. No legal action can be brought against us:
   a. Unless there has been full compliance with all of the terms of this Policy; and
   b. Until the obligation of the "insured" has been determined by final judgment or by agreement signed by us.
2. No person or organization has any right under this Policy to join us as a party to any legal action against an "insured".

K. Termination

1. Cancellation By You

You may cancel this Policy by:

a. Returning it to us; or

b. Giving us advance written notice of the date cancellation is to take effect.

2. Cancellation By Us

We may cancel this Policy as stated below by letting you know in writing of the date cancellation takes effect. This cancellation notice may be delivered to you or mailed to you at your mailing address shown in the Declarations.

Proof of mailing will be sufficient proof of notice.

a. When you have not paid the premium, we may cancel at any time by letting you know at least 10 days before the date cancellation takes effect.

b. When this Policy has been in effect for less than 60 days and is not a renewal with us, we may cancel for any reason by letting you know at least 10 days before the date cancellation takes effect.

c. When this Policy has been in effect for 60 days or more, or at any time if it is a renewal with us, we may cancel by letting you know at least 30 days before the date cancellation takes effect.

3. Nonrenewal

We may elect not to renew this Policy. We may do so by delivering to you, or mailing to you at your mailing address shown in the Declarations, written notice at least 30 days before the expiration date of this Policy. Proof of mailing will be sufficient proof of notice.

4. Other Termination Provisions

a. When this Policy is canceled, the premium for the period from the date of cancellation to the expiration date will be refunded pro rata.

b. If the return premium is not refunded with the notice of cancellation or when this Policy is returned to us, we will refund it within a reasonable time after the date cancellation takes effect.

L. Transfer Of Your Interest In This Policy

1. Your rights and duties under this Policy may not be assigned without our written consent. However, if you die, coverage will be provided for:
   a. The surviving spouse if resident in the same household at the time of death. Coverage applies to the spouse as if a named insured shown in the Declarations;
   b. Any member of your household who is an "insured" at the time of your death, but only while a resident of the residence premises; or
   c. The legal representative of the deceased person as if a named insured shown in the Declarations. This applies only with respect to the representative's legal responsibility to maintain or use your "autos" or the residence premises shown in the Declarations.
2. Coverage will only be provided until the end of the policy period.

M. Waiver Or Change Of Policy Provisions

This Policy contains all the agreements between you and us. Its terms may not be changed or waived except by endorsement issued by us. If a change requires a premium adjustment, we will adjust the premium as of the effective date of the change.

THIS IS A LEGAL CONTRACT
-- PLEASE READ IT CAREFULLY --

PERSONAL UMBRELLA LIABILITY COVERAGE

The following Table of Contents shows how this policy is organized. It will help "you" locate particular sections of this form.

TABLE OF CONTENTS

A state-specific amendatory endorsement applies to this policy. Other endorsements and schedules may also apply. They are identified on the "declarations".

Words and phrases that have special meaning are shown in quotation marks. The special meanings for these words and phrases are set forth in Definitions.

AGREEMENT

This policy, subject to all of its "terms", provides the described insurance coverages during the policy period. In return "you" must pay the required premium.

DEFINITIONS

1. The words "you" and "your" mean the person or persons named as the insured on the "declarations". This includes "your" spouse if a resident of "your" household.

2. The words "we", "us", and "our" mean the company providing this insurance.

3. "Aircraft" means an apparatus or a device designed or used for flight, but this does not include:

   a. a model aircraft that is not designed or used to carry people or cargo;

   b. a "hovercraft"; or

   c. a model hovercraft that is not designed or used to carry people or cargo.

4. "Bodily injury" means bodily harm to a person and includes sickness, disease, or death. This also includes required care and loss of services.

   However, "bodily injury" does not mean bodily harm, sickness, disease, or death that arises out of mental or emotional injury, suffering, or distress that does not result from actual physical injury to a person.

5. "Business" means:

   a. a trade, a profession, or an occupation, including farming, all whether full time, part time, or occasional. This includes the leasing or rental of property to others; or

   b. any other activity undertaken for money or other compensation, but this does not include:

      1) providing care services to a relative of an "insured";
      2) providing services for the care of persons who are not relatives of an "insured" and for which the only compensation is the mutual exchange of like services;
      3) a volunteer activity for which:

         a) an "insured" receives no compensation; or
         b) an "insured's" only compensation is the reimbursement of expenses incurred to carry out the activity; or

      4) an activity not described in 1) through 3) above for which no "insured's" total compensation for the 12 month period just before the first day of this policy period was more than $2,500.

6. "Declarations" means all pages labeled declarations, supplemental declarations, or schedule that pertain to this policy.

7. "Domestic employee" means a person employed by an "insured", or a person leased to an "insured" under a contract or an agreement with a labor leasing firm, to perform duties that relate to the use or care of an "insured premises". This includes a person who performs duties of a similar nature elsewhere for an "insured", provided such duties are not in connection with an "insured's" "business".

   However, "domestic employee" does not include a person who is furnished to an "insured":

   a. as a temporary substitute for a permanent "domestic employee" who is on leave; or

   b. to meet seasonal or short-term workloads.

8. "Employee" means a person employed by an "insured", or a person leased to an "insured" under a contract or an agreement with a labor leasing firm, to perform duties other than those performed by a "domestic employee".

9. "Fungi" means any kind or form of fungus, including but not limited to mildew and mold, and any chemical, matter, or compound produced or released by a fungus, including but not limited to toxins, spores, fragments, and metabolites such as microbial volatile organic compounds.

10. "Household member" means:

    a. "your" relatives if residents of "your" household;

    b. "your" relatives under the age of 25 years who:

        1) are financially dependent upon "you";
        2) are students enrolled in school full time, as defined by the school; and
        3) were residents of "your" household just before moving out to attend school;

    c. persons, other than "your" relatives, under the age of 21 years who:

        1) reside in "your" household; and
        2) are in "your" care or in the care of "your" resident relatives;

    d. persons, other than "your" relatives, under the age of 21 years who:

        1) are in "your" care or in the care of "your" resident relatives;
        2) are students enrolled in school full time, as defined by the school; and
        3) were residents of "your" household just before moving out to attend school;

    e. an "insured", other than a person described in a. through d. above, who:

        1) lives with "you";
        2) is a member of "your" household; and
        3) is not a guest, "domestic employee", "employee", tenant, or roomer or boarder; and

    f. an "insured" under the age of 21 years, other than a person described in a. through d. above, who lives with and is in the legal custody of a person described in e. above.

11. "Hovercraft" means a self-propelled motorized ground effect machine or air cushion vehicle designed or used to travel over land or water. This includes, but is not limited to, a flarecraft.

    However, "hovercraft" does not include:

    a. a model hovercraft that is not designed or used to carry people or cargo;

    b. an "aircraft";

    c. a model aircraft that is not designed or used to carry people or cargo;

    d. a "motorized vehicle";

    e. a "watercraft"; or

    f. a model watercraft that is not designed or used to carry people or cargo.

12. Except as stated within this definition, "insured" means all persons or entities granted status as an insured in "underlying insurance", but only to the extent such status is granted in such "underlying insurance".

    No person is an "insured" with respect to the use of a "motorized vehicle" or "watercraft" unless that person has a reasonable expectation that he or she has a right to such use. However, this does not apply to the use of a "motorized vehicle" or "watercraft" that "you" own, or a "motorized vehicle" that "you" lease under a written agreement for a continuous period of at least six months, by a person who is:

    a. "your" relative and a resident of "your" household;

    b. "your" relative under the age of 25 years who:

        1) is financially dependent upon "you";
        2) is a student enrolled in school full time, as defined by the school; and

3) was a resident of "your" household just before moving out to attend school;

c. under the age of 21 years and who:

1) is not "your" relative;
2) resides in "your" household; and
3) is in "your" care or in the care of "your" resident relatives; or

d. under the age of 21 years and who:

1) is not "your" relative;
2) is in "your" care or in the care of "your" resident relatives;
3) is a student enrolled in school full time, as defined by the school; and
4) was a resident of "your" household just before moving out to attend school.

The phrase an "insured", wherever it appears in this policy, means one or more "insureds".

13. "Insured premises" means all premises covered by "underlying insurance".

14. "Limit" means amount of insurance.

15. "Motorized vehicle" means:

a. a self-propelled land or amphibious vehicle, regardless of method of surface contact, but this does not include a:

1) "hovercraft";
2) model hovercraft that is not designed or used to carry people or cargo;
3) "watercraft"; or
4) model watercraft that is not designed or used to carry people or cargo; or

b. a trailer or semitrailer that:

1) is attached to or being carried on or towed by; or
2) becomes detached while being carried on or towed by;

a vehicle described in a. above.

16. "Occurrence" means an accident, including repeated exposures to similar conditions, that results in "bodily injury" or "property damage" during the policy period.

17. "Personal injury" means injury that arises out of one or more of the following offenses:

a. false arrest, detention, or imprisonment;

b. malicious prosecution;

c. wrongful entry into, wrongful eviction from, or invasion of the right of private occupancy of a room, dwelling, or premises that a person occupies, if such offense is committed by or on behalf of the owner, landlord, or lessor of the room, dwelling, or premises; or

d. oral or written publication, including electronic publication, of material that:

1) slanders or libels a person or an organization;
2) disparages a person's or an organization's goods, products, or services; or
3) violates a person's right of privacy.

18. "Pollutant" means:

a. any solid, liquid, gaseous, thermal, or radioactive irritant or contaminant, including acids, alkalis, chemicals, fumes, smoke, soot, vapor, and waste. Waste includes materials to be disposed of as well as recycled, reclaimed, or reconditioned; and

b. electrical, magnetic, or electromagnetic particles or fields, whether visible or invisible, and sound.

19. "Property damage" means:

a. physical injury to or destruction of tangible property; or

b. the loss of use of tangible property whether or not it is physically damaged.

AAIS
PU 0001 10 11
Page 5 of 16

20. "Suit" means any civil proceeding in a court of law in which damages because of "bodily injury", "personal injury", or "property damage" to which this insurance applies are sought.

    "Suit" also includes arbitration proceedings in which damages for "bodily injury", "personal injury", or "property damage" are claimed and to which an "insured" must submit or does submit with "our" consent, or any other alternative dispute resolution proceeding in which such damages are claimed and to which an "insured" does submit with "our" consent.

21. "Terms" means all provisions, limitations, exclusions, conditions, "declarations", and definitions used in this policy.

22. "Underlying insurance" means the liability insurance coverage provided under policies shown in the Schedule of Underlying Insurance on the "declarations" for the "limits" and policy periods indicated. It includes any policies issued to replace those policies during the term of this policy that provide:

    a. at least the same "limits"; and

    b. the same hazards insured against, except as modified by general program revisions or as agreed to by "us" in writing.

23. "Underlying insurer" means any insurer who issues a policy of "underlying insurance".

24. "Watercraft" means an apparatus or a device primarily designed to be propelled on or in water by engine, motor, or wind, but this does not include:

    a. a model watercraft that is not designed or used to carry people or cargo;

    b. a "hovercraft";

    c. a model hovercraft that is not designed or used to carry people or cargo;

    d. a "motorized vehicle";

    e. an "aircraft"; or

    f. a model aircraft that is not designed or used to carry people or cargo.

PRINCIPAL COVERAGE

"We" pay, up to the "limit" that applies, those sums for which an "insured" is legally liable because of "bodily injury", "personal injury", or "property damage" to which this Personal Umbrella Liability Coverage applies.

No other obligation or liability to pay sums or perform acts or services is covered unless explicitly provided for under Defense Coverage.

Subject to the Exclusions, this insurance applies only to:

1. "bodily injury" and "property damage" that is caused by an "occurrence"; and

2. "personal injury" arising from an offense committed during the policy period.

DEFENSE COVERAGE

1. "We" have the right to defend, investigate, and settle any claim or "suit" seeking damages covered by this policy. "We" may elect at any time to participate with an "insured" and with any "underlying insurer" or other insurer in the defense, investigation, and settlement of any claim or "suit" arising out of an "occurrence" or an offense that, in "our" opinion, may involve damages to which this policy may apply. Any such defense will be provided at "our" expense by counsel that "we" choose.

   However, "we" have no obligation to share in or contribute to any costs or expenses incurred by any "underlying insurer" or other insurer.

2. "We" have the duty to defend any claim or "suit" seeking damages to which this insurance applies, but only with respect to damages:

   a. covered by "underlying insurance" or any other valid and collectible insurance available to the "insured" except for exhaustion of a "limit" of such "underlying insurance" or other insurance by the payment of losses; or

   b. not covered by "underlying insurance" or any other valid and collectible insurance available to the "insured".

      However, "we" have no duty to defend a claim or "suit" seeking damages for an amount that does not exceed the Personal Umbrella Liability Coverage Retained Limit shown on the "declarations".

   Such defense will be provided at "our" expense by counsel that "we" choose.

   "Our" duty to defend ends when "we" have paid an amount equal to the "limit" that applies as a result of a judgment or written settlement.

   If "we" are prevented by law or otherwise prevented from carrying out this agreement, "we" will pay the "insured" for any expense incurred with "our" written consent.

3. "We" pay for:

   a. the costs incurred by "us" and the costs taxed to an "insured" in a "suit" "we" defend;

   b. the premiums on required bonds in a "suit" "we" defend, but only for bond amounts up to the "limit" that applies. "We" are not required to apply for or furnish bonds;

   c. the necessary costs incurred by an "insured" at "our" request for assisting "us" in the investigation or defense of a claim or "suit". This includes up to $250 per day, per "insured", for the actual loss of earnings, but not loss of other income, for time spent away from work at "our" request;

   d. the interest on "our" share of the judgment that accrues after the entry of the judgment, but ending when "we" tender, pay, or deposit in court that part of the judgment that does not exceed the "limit" that applies; and

   e. prejudgment interest awarded against an "insured" on that part of the judgment "we" pay. If "we" offer to pay the "limit" that applies, "we" will not pay any prejudgment interest based on that period of time after the offer.

   These payments will not reduce the "limit" that applies as described under How Much We Pay.

EXCLUSIONS

This Personal Umbrella Liability Coverage does not apply to:

1. "bodily injury", "personal injury", or "property damage" arising out of or in any way related to a "business":

   a. conducted from any part of a premises, or vacant land, owned by or leased or rented to an "insured"; or

   b. undertaken by an "insured", regardless of location;

   whether or not the "business" is owned or operated by an "insured" or employs an "insured" and whether or not the "bodily injury", "personal injury", or "property damage" is covered by "underlying insurance" at the time of the "occurrence" or offense.

This includes but is not limited to "bodily injury", "personal injury", or "property damage" arising out of an act or a failure to act, regardless of its circumstance, involving a service or duty owed, promised, provided, or implied to be provided because of the nature of the "business".

However, this exclusion does not apply:

a. with respect to an "insured premises" normally occupied by "your" household:

   1) to the occasional rental or holding for rental for use as a residence of that part of the "insured premises" normally occupied solely by "your" household; or
   2) to the leasing or rental or holding for lease or rental for use as a residence of part of the "insured premises" not normally occupied solely by "your" household, but only if no family unit houses more than two roomers or boarders;

b. to the leasing or rental or holding for lease or rental, in whole or in part, of an "insured premises", other than an "insured premises" described in a.1) or a.2) above, for use as a residence;

c. to the leasing or rental or holding for lease or rental of part of an "insured premises" for use as a school, studio, office, or private garage;

d. to the "business" activities of an "insured" under the age of 21 years, but only if such "insured" is involved in a part-time or occasional, self-employed "business" that does not employ others and the "bodily injury", "property damage", or "personal injury" arises out of activities related to that "business";

e. to civic or public activities performed by an "insured" for no compensation or for which the only compensation is the reimbursement of expenses incurred to carry out the activity; or

f. to the use of a "motorized vehicle", but only to the extent that such use is covered by "underlying insurance" at the time of the "occurrence" or offense or would have been covered but for the exhaustion of its "limits".

   However, regardless of the terms of the "underlying insurance", this Personal Umbrella Liability Coverage does not apply to "bodily injury", "personal injury", or "property damage" arising out of the use of a "motorized vehicle" as a public or livery conveyance, other than a share-the-expense car pool.

2. "bodily injury", "personal injury", or "property damage" arising out of the rendering of or the failing to render a professional service.

3. "bodily injury", "personal injury", or "property damage" arising out of an "insured's" service as an officer or a member of a board of directors.

   However, this exclusion does not apply to "bodily injury", "personal injury", or "property damage" arising out of an "insured's" service as an officer or a member of a board of directors for a not for profit organization:

   a. that does not employ the "insured", or lease the "insured" under a contract or an agreement with a labor leasing firm; and

   b. for which the "insured" is not compensated.

   With respect to this exclusion and the exception stated above, reimbursement of expenses incurred is not considered compensation.

4. "bodily injury", "personal injury", or "property damage" that arises out of the actual, alleged, or threatened discharge, dispersal, disposal, emission, escape, leaching, leakage, migration, release, seepage, or spillage of "pollutants" into or upon land, water, or air.

However, this exclusion does not apply to:

a. "bodily injury" or "property damage" that arises out of the heat, smoke, or fumes of a fire on an "insured premises" that becomes uncontrollable or breaks out from where it was intended to be; or

b. "bodily injury" or "property damage" that arises out of the actual, alleged, or threatened discharge, dispersal, disposal, emission, escape, leaching, leakage, migration, release, seepage, or spillage of "pollutants" from a "motorized vehicle", but only to the extent that such "bodily injury" or "property damage" is covered by "underlying insurance" at the time of the "occurrence" or would have been covered but for the exhaustion of its "limits".

5. "bodily injury", "personal injury", or "property damage" that arises out of the transmission of a communicable disease by an "insured".

6. "bodily injury", "personal injury", or "property damage" that arises out of sexual molestation.

7. "bodily injury", "personal injury", or "property damage" that arises out of physical or mental abuse.

8. "bodily injury", "personal injury", or "property damage" that arises out of corporal punishment.

9. "bodily injury", "personal injury", or "property damage" that arises out of the use, sale, manufacture, delivery, transfer, or possession by any person of a Controlled Substance as defined by the Federal Food and Drug Law at 21 U.S.C.A. Sections 811 and 812, including any amendments. Controlled Substances include but are not limited to cocaine, LSD, marijuana, and all narcotic or hallucinogenic drugs.

   However, this exclusion does not apply to the extent that such "bodily injury", "personal injury", or "property damage" is covered by "underlying insurance" at the time of the "occurrence" or offense or would have been covered but for the exhaustion of its "limits".

10. "bodily injury", "personal injury", or "property damage" that arises out of electronic aggression, including but not limited to harassment or bullying committed:

    a. by means of an electronic forum, including but not limited to a blog, an electronic bulletin board, an electronic chat room, a gripe site, a social networking site, a web site, or a weblog; or

    b. by other electronic means, including but not limited to email, instant messaging, or text messaging.

11. "bodily injury", "personal injury", or "property damage" that arises directly or indirectly out of an actual or alleged violation of:

    a. the Telephone Consumer Protection Act of 1991 (TCPA), including any amendments, or any similar federal, state, or local law, ordinance, statute, or regulation;

    b. the CAN-Spam Act of 2003, including any amendments, or any similar federal, state, or local law, ordinance, statute, or regulation; or

    c. any federal, state, or local law, ordinance, statute, or regulation, other than the TCPA or the CAN-Spam Act of 2003, that limits or prohibits the communicating, transmitting, sending, or distribution of material or information.

12. "bodily injury" or "personal injury" to "you" or a "household member".

    This exclusion also applies to any claim made or "suit" brought against "you" or a "household member" by a person seeking reimbursement of or contribution toward damages for which that person may be liable because of "bodily injury" or "personal injury" to "you" or a "household member".

13. "bodily injury" or "property damage" arising out of:

    a. the ownership of "aircraft" or "hovercraft" by an "insured" or the leasing or renting of "aircraft" or "hovercraft" by an "insured" from another;

    b. the operation, maintenance, use, occupancy, loading, or unloading of "aircraft" or "hovercraft" by any person;

    c. the entrustment or loaning of "aircraft" or "hovercraft" by an "insured" to any person; or

    d. an "insured's" negligent supervision of or failure to supervise any person with respect to "aircraft" or "hovercraft".

    However, this exclusion does not apply to "bodily injury" to a "domestic employee" arising out of and in the course of his or her employment by an "insured".

14. "bodily injury" or "property damage" for which an "insured" is vicariously liable if the "bodily injury" or "property damage" arises out of the actions of a child or minor with respect to:

    a. "aircraft"; or

    b. "hovercraft".

    This applies whether or not such liability is imposed by law.

15. "bodily injury" or "property damage" arising out of:

    a. the ownership of a "motorized vehicle" by an "insured" or the leasing or renting of a "motorized vehicle" by an "insured" from another;

    b. the operation, maintenance, use, occupancy, loading, or unloading of a "motorized vehicle" by any person;

    c. the entrustment or loaning of a "motorized vehicle" by an "insured" to any person; or

    d. an "insured's" negligent supervision of or failure to supervise any person with respect to a "motorized vehicle".

    Except as stated in the following paragraph, this exclusion does not apply to the extent that such "bodily injury" or "property damage" is covered by "underlying insurance" at the time of the "occurrence" or would have been covered but for the exhaustion of its "limits".

    Regardless of the terms of the "underlying insurance", this Personal Umbrella Liability Coverage does not provide automobile no fault or any similar coverage, uninsured motorists coverage or underinsured motorists coverage or any similar coverage, or automobile medical expense, automobile medical payments, or any similar coverage.

16. "bodily injury" or "property damage" arising out of:

    a. the ownership of a "watercraft" by an "insured" or the leasing or renting of a "watercraft" by an "insured" from another;

    b. the operation, maintenance, use, occupancy, loading, or unloading of a "watercraft" by any person;

    c. the entrustment or loaning of a "watercraft" by an "insured" to any person; or

    d. an "insured's" negligent supervision of or failure to supervise any person with respect to a "watercraft".

    Except as stated in the following paragraphs, this exclusion does not apply to the extent that such "bodily injury" or "property damage" is covered by "underlying insurance" at the time of the "occurrence" or would have been covered but for the exhaustion of its "limits".

Regardless of the terms of the "underlying insurance", this Personal Umbrella Liability Coverage does not apply to "bodily injury" or "property damage" arising out of the use of "watercraft" in or in the practice or the preparation for any prearranged or organized racing, speed, or stunt activities or contests. This does not apply to "watercraft" used in predicted log cruises or to sailing vessels.

Regardless of the terms of the "underlying insurance", this Personal Umbrella Liability Coverage does not provide uninsured boaters coverage or underinsured boaters coverage or any similar coverage, or boaters medical expense, boaters medical payments, or any similar coverage.

17. "bodily injury" or "property damage" for which an "insured" is vicariously liable if the "bodily injury" or "property damage" arises out of the actions of a child or minor with respect to:

    a. a "motorized vehicle"; or

    b. "watercraft".

    This applies whether or not such liability is imposed by law.

    However, this exclusion does not apply to the extent that such liability is covered by "underlying insurance" at the time of the "occurrence" or would have been covered but for the exhaustion of its "limits".

18. "bodily injury" or "property damage" arising out of the use of a "motorized vehicle" in or in the practice or the preparation for a prearranged or organized racing, speed, pulling or pushing, demolition, or stunt activity or contest.

19. "bodily injury" or "property damage" caused directly or indirectly by:

    a. war, including undeclared or civil war;

    b. warlike action by a military force, including action in hindering or defending against an actual or expected attack, by any government, sovereign, or other authority using military personnel or other agents; or

    c. insurrection, rebellion, revolution, usurped power, or action taken by governmental authority in hindering or defending against any of these.

    Discharge of a nuclear weapon is deemed a warlike action even if it is accidental.

20. "bodily injury" or "property damage" arising out of an "occurrence" for which an "insured" is also an insured under a nuclear energy liability policy or would be an insured under a nuclear energy liability policy but for the exhaustion of its "limits". (A nuclear energy liability policy is a policy issued by Mutual Atomic Energy Liability Underwriters, Nuclear Energy Liability Insurance Association, or Nuclear Insurance Association of Canada or their successors.)

21. actual or alleged "bodily injury" that arises directly or indirectly out of the ingestion, inhalation, or absorption of lead in any form.

22. "bodily injury" to a person, including a "domestic employee", if:

    a. the "insured" has a workers' compensation policy covering the injury; or

    b. benefits are payable or are required to be provided by an "insured" because of the existence, application, or enforcement of any provisions of any workers' compensation, non-occupational disability, occupational disease, or like law.

23. "personal injury" arising out of lead in any form.

24. "personal injury" arising out of an act committed by or directed by an "insured" who knew that the act would violate the rights of another and would result in "personal injury".

25. "personal injury" sustained by any person as a result of an offense directly or indirectly related to such person's employment by an "insured", or leasing by an "insured" under a contract or an agreement with a labor leasing firm.

26. "personal injury" arising out of oral or written publication, including electronic publication, of material that was first published before the effective date of this insurance.

27. "personal injury" arising out of oral or written publication, including electronic publication, of material by or at the direction of an "insured" who knew that the publication was false.

28. "personal injury" arising directly or indirectly, in whole or in part, from the actual, alleged, or threatened ingestion of, inhalation of, contact with, exposure to, existence of, presence of, or any activity of bacteria, "fungi", wet rot, or dry rot.

29. "personal injury" arising out of a criminal act committed by or directed by an "insured".

30. "personal injury" arising out of electronic chat rooms, bulletin boards, gripe sites, social networking sites, or other forums that an "insured" hosts, owns, or has the control or authority to update.

    However, this exclusion does not apply to "personal injury" arising out of content posted by an "insured" or provided by an "insured" for posting by others to a web site, weblog, blog, or other electronic forum.

31. "property damage" to property owned by an "insured".

    This exclusion also applies to cost or expense for measures performed on property owned by an "insured" to prevent:

    a. injury to a person; or

    b. damage to property of others;

    on or away from an "insured premises", whether such cost or expense is incurred by an "insured" or others.

32. actual or alleged "property damage" that arises directly or indirectly out of any form of lead.

33. any liability of anyone who is an "insured" under this policy for "bodily injury" or "property damage" that is:

    a. expected by, directed by, or intended by any "insured";

    b. the result of a criminal act of any "insured"; or

    c. the result of an intentional and malicious act by or at the direction of any "insured".

    There is no coverage for anyone who is an "insured" under this policy for any "bodily injury" or "property damage" arising out of any of the acts described in a., b., or c. above regardless of the theory of relief pursued, asserted, or claimed against the person or entity seeking coverage under this policy.

    This exclusion applies even if the "bodily injury" or "property damage" that occurs is different than what was expected, directed, or intended or is suffered by persons, entities, or property not expected, directed, or intended.

    However, this exclusion does not apply:

    a. to "bodily injury" or "property damage" that arises out of the use of reasonable force by an "insured" to protect people or property; or

    b. to the extent that such "bodily injury" or "property damage" is covered by "underlying insurance" at the time of the "occurrence" or would have been covered but for the exhaustion of its "limits".

34. liability under a contract or an agreement entered into by an "insured".

    However, this exclusion does not apply to the extent that such liability is covered by "underlying insurance" at the time of the "occurrence" or offense or would have been covered but for the exhaustion of its "limits".

35. liability for any assessment levied by a homeowners, condominium, mobile-homeowners, or similar residential association.

36. any loss, cost, or expense arising out of any:

    a. request, demand, order, or statutory or regulatory requirement that an "insured" or others test for, monitor, clean up, remove, contain, treat, detoxify, neutralize, or in any way respond to or assess the effects of "pollutants"; or

    b. claim or suit by or on behalf of any governmental body or authority relating to testing for, monitoring, cleaning up, removing, containing, treating, detoxifying, neutralizing, or in any way responding to or assessing the effects of "pollutants".

    However, this exclusion does not apply to such loss, cost, or expense arising out of a "motorized vehicle", but only to the extent that the loss, cost, or expense is covered by "underlying insurance" at the time of the "occurrence" or would have been covered but for the exhaustion of its "limits".

37. any loss, cost, or expense arising out of any:

    a. request, demand, order, or statutory or regulatory requirement that an "insured" or others test for, monitor, clean up, remove, contain, treat, detoxify, neutralize, or in any way respond to or assess the effects of lead; or

    b. claim or suit by or on behalf of any governmental body or authority relating to testing for, monitoring, cleaning up, removing, containing, treating, detoxifying, neutralizing, or in any way responding to or assessing the effects of lead.

38. loss, cost, or expense arising out of any:

    a. request, demand, order, or statutory or regulatory requirement that an "insured" or others test for, monitor, clean up, remove, contain, treat, detoxify, neutralize, or in any way respond to or assess the effects of bacteria, "fungi", wet rot, or dry rot; or

    b. claim or suit by or on behalf of any governmental body or authority relating to testing for, monitoring, cleaning up, removing, containing, treating, detoxifying, neutralizing, or in any way responding to or assessing the effects of bacteria, "fungi", wet rot, or dry rot.

39. sickness, disease, or death of a "domestic employee" unless a written notice is received by "us" within 36 months after the end of the policy period in which the injury occurred.

WHAT MUST BE DONE IN CASE OF LOSS

The following duties apply when there has been an "occurrence" or offense to which this insurance may apply. These duties must be performed by "you" or another "insured". "You" must assist "us" by seeing that they are performed.

"We" are not obligated to provide the Personal Umbrella Liability Coverage described in this policy if these duties are not performed.

1. The "insured" must cooperate with the "underlying insurers" as required by the terms of their policies and comply with all terms and conditions of those policies.

2. Written notice must be given to "us" or "our" agent as soon as is practical. The notice must state:

    a. "your" name and the policy number;

    b. reasonably available information regarding the time, location, and other details of the "occurrence" or offense; and

    c. the names and addresses of all known potential claimants and witnesses.

3. **Volunteer Payments** -- Any:

   a. payments made;

   b. rewards paid or offered; or

   c. obligations or other costs assumed;

   by an "insured" will be at the "insured's" own cost.

4. **Cooperation** -- The "insured" must cooperate with "us" in the investigation, defense, or settlement of a claim or "suit".

5. **Notices, Demands, And Legal Papers** -- The "insured" must promptly give "us" copies of all notices, demands, and legal papers that relate to the "occurrence" or offense.

6. **Assistance With Claims And Suits** -- At "our" request, the "insured" must help "us":

   a. to settle a claim;

   b. to enforce the right of recovery or indemnification against all parties who may be liable to an "insured";

   c. to conduct "suits". This includes being at trials and hearings;

   d. in the securing of and giving of evidence; and

   e. in obtaining the attendance of all witnesses.

HOW MUCH WE PAY

1. The Personal Umbrella Liability Coverage Aggregate Limit is the most "we" pay for the sum of all damages for "bodily injury", "personal injury", and "property damage":

   a. subject to an aggregate "limit" in "underlying insurance"; and

   b. not excluded by this policy.

   The Personal Umbrella Liability Coverage Aggregate Limit is equal to the Personal Umbrella Liability Coverage Limit.

   The Personal Umbrella Liability Coverage Aggregate Limit applies separately to each consecutive 12-month period beginning with the inception date shown on the "declarations" for this Personal Umbrella Liability Coverage. It also applies separately to any remaining policy period of less than 12 months, unless the Personal Umbrella Liability Coverage was extended after it was written. In that case, the additional period will be considered part of the last preceding period for the purpose of determining "limits".

2. With respect to "bodily injury" and "property damage" to which this Personal Umbrella Liability Coverage applies, the Personal Umbrella Liability Coverage Limit shown on the "declarations" is the most "we" pay for loss for each "occurrence". This applies regardless of the number of:

   a. persons insured under this policy;

   b. parties who sustain injury or damage;

   c. claims made or "suits" brought;

   d. vehicles, "watercraft", trailers, or semitrailers involved in an accident; or

   e. policy periods involved.

   All "bodily injury" and "property damage" arising out of any one accident or out of repeated exposures to similar conditions will be considered one "occurrence".

   The Personal Umbrella Liability Coverage Limit is subject to the Personal Umbrella Liability Coverage Aggregate Limit as set forth in 1. above.

3. With respect to "personal injury" to which this Personal Umbrella Liability Coverage applies, the Personal Umbrella Liability Coverage Limit shown on the "declarations" is the most "we" pay for all "personal injury" sustained by any one person or organization. This applies regardless of the number of:

   a. persons insured under this policy;

   b. claims made or "suits" brought; or

   c. offenses committed during the policy period.

   The Personal Umbrella Liability Coverage Limit is subject to the Personal Umbrella Liability Coverage Aggregate Limit as set forth in 1. above.

4. The Personal Umbrella Liability Coverage provided by this policy applies separately to each "insured", but this does not increase the Personal Umbrella Liability Coverage Aggregate Limit or:

   a. with respect to "bodily injury" and "property damage" to which this Personal Umbrella Liability Coverage applies, the "limit" that applies for any one "occurrence"; and

   b. with respect to "personal injury" to which this Personal Umbrella Liability Coverage applies, the "limit" that applies to "personal injury" sustained by any one person or organization.

EXCESS INSURANCE

1. **Other Insurance** -- The insurance provided by this policy is excess over "underlying insurance", whether or not valid and collectible, and any other valid and collectible insurance available to the "insured", except insurance that is specifically purchased by the "insured" as excess insurance over the insurance provided by this policy.

   If there is no "underlying insurance" or valid and collectible insurance available to the "insured" with respect to an "occurrence" or offense to which the insurance provided by this policy applies, then this insurance will apply as excess over the Personal Umbrella Liability Coverage Retained Limit shown on the "declarations", except when:

   a. the "underlying insurer" is bankrupt or insolvent as stated below under item 3., Bankruptcy Of Underlying Insurer; or

   b. "you" fail to maintain "underlying insurance" as stated under Condition 7., Maintenance Of Underlying Insurance.

2. **Failure To Maintain Underlying Insurance** -- If "you" fail to maintain "underlying insurance" as required by Condition 7., Maintenance Of Underlying Insurance, the insurance provided by this policy will not replace such "underlying insurance" but will apply as if the required "limits" of such "underlying insurance" were valid and collectible.

3. **Bankruptcy Of Underlying Insurer** -- In the event of bankruptcy or insolvency of any "underlying insurer", the insurance provided by this policy will not replace such "underlying insurance", but will apply as if the "limits" of such "underlying insurance" were valid and collectible.

CONDITIONS

1. **Appeals** -- If an "insured" or "underlying insurer" elects not to appeal a judgment in excess of the "limit" of any "underlying insurance", "we" may elect to make such appeal. If "we" so elect, "we" will be liable, in addition to the applicable "limit", for all expenses "we" incur that pertain to such appeal.

2. **Bankruptcy Of An Insured** -- Bankruptcy or insolvency of an "insured" does not:

    a. relieve "us" of "our" obligations under this policy; or

    b. make this policy primary in the event that such bankruptcy or insolvency results in the "insured" being unable to satisfy "underlying insurance" "limit" requirements or the Personal Umbrella Liability Coverage Retained Limit.

3. **Change, Modification, Or Waiver of Policy Terms**

    a. A waiver or change of the "terms" of this policy must be issued by "us" in writing to be valid.

    b. If "we" adopt a revision that broadens coverage under this edition of "our" policy without an additional premium, the broadened coverage will apply to "your" policy as of the date "we" adopt the revision in the state in which "your" mailing address shown on the "declarations" is located. This applies only to revisions adopted within 60 days prior to or during the policy period shown on the "declarations".

        However, this does not apply to revisions adopted as part of an overall program revision that both broadens and restricts coverage, whether "we" bring about the program revision by introducing:

        1) a subsequent edition of "our" policy; or
        2) an endorsement that amends "our" policy.

4. **Conformity With Statute** -- "Terms" in conflict with the laws of the state in which "your" mailing address shown on the "declarations" is located are changed to conform to such laws.

5. **Inspections** -- "We" have the right, but are not obligated, to inspect "your" property and operations. This inspection may be made by "us" or may be made on "our" behalf. An inspection or its resulting advice or report does not warrant that "your" property or operations are safe, healthful, or in compliance with laws, rules, or regulations. Inspections or reports are for "our" benefit only.

6. **Legal Action Against Us** -- No legal action may be brought against "us" unless:

    a. all the "terms" of this policy have been complied with; and

    b. the amount of the "insured's" liability has been fixed by:

        1) a final judgment against the "insured" as a result of a trial; or
        2) a written agreement of the "insured", the claimant, and "us".

    No person has a right under this policy to join "us" or implead "us" in actions that are brought to fix the liability of an "insured".

7. **Maintenance Of Underlying Insurance** -- "You" must maintain the "underlying insurance" in full force and effect during the term of this policy.

    If any "underlying insurance" is canceled or not renewed and not replaced or is at any time materially changed in "limits" or coverages, "you" must notify "us" within 30 days of the effective date of such cancellation, nonrenewal, or change. "We" will not be liable under this policy for more than "we" would have been liable if that "underlying insurance" had not been terminated or had been kept at its original "limits" or coverages.

    Reduction or exhaustion of any aggregate "limit" in any "underlying insurance" by payments for judgments, settlements, or expenses for "occurrences" or offenses during the policy period of this policy will not be a failure to maintain "underlying insurance" in full force and effect.

    No statement contained in this condition limits "our" right to cancel or not renew this policy.

8. **Misrepresentation, Concealment, Or Fraud** -- "We" do not provide coverage for any "insured" if, before or after a loss:

   a. an "insured" has willfully concealed or misrepresented a material fact or circumstance that relates to this insurance or the subject thereof; or

   b. there has been fraudulent conduct or false swearing by an "insured" with regard to a matter that relates to this insurance or the subject thereof.

   This applies even with respect to an "insured" who was not involved in the concealment, misrepresentation, fraudulent conduct, or false swearing.

9. **Policy Period** -- The policy period is shown on the "declarations".

10. **Subrogation** -- If "we" pay for a loss, "we" may require that the "insured" assign to "us" the right of recovery up to the amount "we" pay. "We" are not liable for a loss if, after the loss, an "insured" impairs "our" right to recover against others. An "insured" may waive his or her right to recover, in writing, and before a loss occurs, without affecting coverage.

    In the event that "we" require such an assignment, the "insured" must:

    a. sign and give to "us" all related documents; and

    b. cooperate with "us".

11. **Transfer Of Your Rights And Duties Under This Policy** -- "Your" rights and duties under this policy may not be transferred without "our" written consent except in the case of "your" death.

    The "terms" in a. and b. below apply if a person named as the insured on the "declarations" dies.

    a. The deceased person's rights and duties will be transferred to:

       1) the surviving spouse, if a resident of the deceased person's household at the time of death;
       2) the legal representative of the deceased person, but only:

          a) with respect to property of the deceased person that is covered by this policy at the time of death; and
          b) while acting within the scope of duties as the deceased person's legal representative; or

       3) anyone having proper, temporary custody of property of the deceased person that is covered by this policy at the time of death, but only with respect to such property and only until the deceased person's legal representative is appointed and qualified.

    b. "Insured" includes an "insured" who is a member of the deceased person's household at the time of the deceased person's death, but only while a resident of an "insured premises" normally occupied by the household of the deceased person.

PERSONAL UMBRELLA LIABILITY FORM – MPL 100 01 12

This Coverage Form provides excess liability insurance over other primary liability insurance policies *you* have that are described in the Umbrella Declarations Page.

THIS COVERAGE FORM INCLUDES:

DEFINITIONS AND WORD MEANINGS

Words shown in *italics* are defined for the purposes of this insurance in the Glossary.

The meanings of other words / phrases not specially defined in this form are to be found in their relevant conventional definitions based on consideration of the context in which they are used in this form.

SECTION I • INSURING AGREEMENT

***We* agree with *you* in consideration of the payment of premium and in reliance upon *your* statements in the Declarations and subject to the Limit of Insurance shown in the Umbrella Declarations, and all the exclusions, terms and conditions of this coverage form as follows:**

A. PERSONAL UMBRELLA LIABILITY COVERAGE

We will pay on behalf of the *insured* the *ultimate net loss* in excess of the *applicable underlying limit,* whether or not collectible, which the *insured* becomes legally obligated to pay as damages because of *bodily injury, property damage* or *personal injury* to which this insurance applies caused by an *occurrence* or offense.

B. DEFENSE OF CLAIMS OR SUITS

1. *We* have no duty to defend any claim or suit that any other insurer has a duty to defend. If *we* elect to join in the defense of such a claim or suit, *we* will pay all expenses *we* incur.

2. *We* will have the right and duty to defend any suit for damages which are payable under this insurance (including damages wholly or partly within the *retained limit)* but which are not payable by an *underlying primary insurance* policy, or any other available insurance, because:

a. Such damages are not covered; or

b. The *underlying primary insurance* has been exhausted by the payment of claims.

3. *We* may investigate and settle any claim or suit in the preceding Paragraph 2, at *our* discretion.

4. *Our* right and duty in the preceding Paragraph 2, end when *we* have used up *our* limit of liability in the payment of judgments or settlements.

5. *We* will pay, with respect to any claim or suit *we* defend in the preceding Paragraph 2:

a. All expenses *we* incur.

b. The cost of bonds to release attachments, but only for bond amounts within *our* limit of liability.

We do not have to furnish these bonds.

c. All reasonable expenses incurred by the *insured* at *our* request to assist *us* in the investigation or defense of the claim or suit, including actual loss of earnings up to $250 a day because of time off from work.

d. All costs taxed against the *insured* in any suit *we* defend.

e. Prejudgment interest awarded against the *insured* on that part of any judgment *we* pay. If *we* make an offer to pay *our* limit of liability, *we* will not pay any prejudgment interest imposed or earned after the date of such offer.

f. All interest earned on the full amount of any judgment after entry of the judgment and before *we* have paid, offered to pay, or deposited in court that part of the judgment that is within *our* limit of liability.

These payments will not reduce the limit of liability.

SECTION II • LIABILITY NOT INSURED / EXCLUSIONS

***We* do not provide insurance for any sort of damages, expenses, liability, or loss directly or indirectly, wholly or partially, aggravated by, consisting of, or resulting from the following – even if an *occurrence* otherwise covered contributes to such concurrently or in any sequence.**

1. *AIRCRAFT; MOTOR VEHICLES;* WATERCRAFT EXCLUSION

A. *We* do not cover *bodily injury, property damage* or *personal injury* arising out of:

1. The maintenance, operation, ownership, or use (including loading or unloading) of any *aircraft, motor vehicle,* or watercraft owned or operated by, or rented or loaned to, any *insured.*

2. The entrustment to others (whether or not under any form of supervision) of any *aircraft, motor vehicle,* or watercraft; statutory vicarious liability of parents for acts of minors using an *aircraft, motor vehicle,* or watercraft.

B. This exclusion (Paragraph A) does not apply to the extent that coverage for such is provided in *underlying primary insurance.*

But *we* do not cover *bodily injury, property damage* or *personal injury* arising out of newly acquired *aircraft, motor vehicles or watercraft* unless *we* are notified within 30 days of such acquisition.

2. *BUSINESS* ACTIVITIES EXCLUSION

We do not cover *bodily injury, property damage,* or *personal injury* arising out of any *business* activities.

But this exclusion does not apply to the extent that coverage for such activities is provided in *underlying primary insurance.*

3. DIRECTORS' ACTIVITIES EXCLUSION

We do not cover *bodily injury, property damage,* or *personal injury* arising out of activities of an *insured* as an officer or a member of a board of directors of a corporation or organization (this does not apply if such is chartered as a charitable, civic, nonprofit, or religious organization).

4. ***ELECTRONIC AGGRESSION* EXCLUSION**
We do not cover *bodily injury, property damage* or *personal injury* arising out of or resulting from *electronic aggression.*

5. **ENDANGERMENT OR HARM EXCLUSION**
We do not cover *bodily injury* or *property damage,* whether or not expected or intended by the *insured:*
   - **A.** Which is a consequence of an *insured's* willfully harmful act or knowing endangerment;
   - **B.** Which arises out of the transmission of a communicable disease by an *insured;* or
   - **C.** Which arises out of sexual molestation, corporal punishment, or physical or mental abuse.

6. **FUEL OIL EXCLUSION**
   - **A.** *We* do not cover *property damage* arising out of the actual or threatened discharge, dispersal, disposal, emission, escape, flowing, leaching, leakage, migration, release, seepage or spill of fuel oil regardless of where or how such may take place.
   - **B.** *We* do not cover any cost, expense, liability, or loss arising out of any of the following:
     1. Any demand, directive, order, or request that any *insured* or others clean up, contain, detoxify, monitor, neutralize, remove, test for, treat, or in any way assess the effects of or respond to fuel oil or fuel oil contamination; or
     2. Any claim or suit by, or on behalf of, any governmental authority for damages or reimbursement because of cleaning up, containing, detoxifying, monitoring, neutralizing, removing, testing for, treating, or in any way assessing the effects of or responding to fuel oil or fuel oil contamination.

7. ***FUNGI* / MOLD EXCLUSION**
   - **A.** *We* do not cover *bodily injury or property damage,* resulting from or caused by the actual, alleged, or threatened absorption of, contact with, existence of, exposure to, inhalation of, ingestion of, or presence of any *fungi.*
   - **B.** *We* do not cover any cost, expense, liability or loss arising out of any of the following:
     1. Any demand, directive, order, or request that any *insured* or others clean up, contain, detoxify, monitor, neutralize, remove, test for, or treat, or in any way assess the effects of or respond to *fungi.*
     2. Any claim or suit by, or on behalf of, any governmental authority for damages or reimbursement because of cleaning up, containing, detoxifying, monitoring, neutralizing, removing, testing for, treating, or in any way assessing the effects of or responding to *fungi.*

   However, these exclusions do not apply to *bodily injury* resulting from the ingestion of foods, goods or products intended for human consumption.

   Glossary
   Fungi means any type or form of fungus, mold, mildew, spores, algae, smut, protists, rusts or *rot and decay organisms,* and any similar or related organisms and any mycotoxin, substance, compounds, chemicals, mist or vapor produced by any *fungi* in any form, or any by-products or waste produced by *fungi,* but does not include any *fungi* intended to be edible.

   Rot and decay organisms means any living organism that causes decomposition of physical property.

8. **GOVERNMENTAL AND LEGAL ACTION EXCLUSION**
   - **A.** *We* do not cover *bodily injury, property damage* or *personal injury* arising out of or resulting from:
     1. Any act or condition of war (declared or not), civil war, invasion, insurrection, rebellion, revolution, or seizure of power, including acts done to defend against such acts or conditions, whether actual or expected.
     2. Confiscation or seizure by civil or military authorities under customs or quarantine regulations or laws authorizing such acts.
     3. Violation of any ordinance, regulation or statute that prohibits or limits the communicating, distributing, sending or transmitting of material or information such as the Telephone Consumer Protection Act (TCPA) or the CAN-SPAM Act of 2003, including any amendments or additions to such laws.
     4. Knowing violation of penal law or ordinance committed by, or with the consent of, an *insured.*
     5. The delivery, manufacture, possession, sale, transfer or use by any person of any Controlled Substance as defined by the Federal Food and Drug Law at 21 U.S.C.A. Sections 811 and 812. Controlled Substances include, but are not limited to: cocaine, LSD, marijuana and all narcotic drugs. However, this exclusion does not apply to the legitimate use of prescription drugs by a person following the orders of a licensed physician.
   - **B.** *We* do not cover any fine, pecuniary, or forfeiture to any federal, state or local governmental unit.
   - **C.** *We* do not cover any exemplary or punitive damages.

9. **INJURY TO *INSUREDS* EXCLUSION**
We do not cover *bodily injury* or *personal injury* to any *insured.*

10. **NO-FAULT AND SIMILAR LAWS EXCLUSION**
We do not cover *bodily injury, property damage,* or *personal injury* for which benefits are required by law to be provided or made available to an *insured* under any automobile no-fault, uninsured motorist, or underinsured motorist law or similar law.

11. **NONOWNED PROPERTY EXCLUSION**

We do not cover *property damage* to property in the care of, occupied or used by, or rented to, any *insured.*

12. **NUCLEAR LIABILITY EXCLUSION**
We do not cover *bodily injury* or *property damage* with respect to which an *insured* under this insurance is also an insured under any nuclear energy liability policy (or would have been an insured under such but for its termination upon exhaustion of its limits).

A nuclear energy liability policy is one issued by the Nuclear Energy Liability Association, Mutual Atomic Energy Liability Underwriters or Nuclear Insurance Association of Canada, or any of their successors.

13. **OWNED PROPERTY EXCLUSION**
We do not cover *property damage* to property owned by any *insured.*

14. ***PERSONAL INJURY* EXCLUSION**
We do not cover any *personal injury:*
   - **A.** Arising out of oral or written publication of material, if done by or at the direction of the *insured* with knowledge of its falsity; or
   - **B.** Arising out of oral or written publication of material whose first publication took place before the beginning of the policy period. All *personal injury* arising out of publication of the same or similar material subsequent to the beginning of the policy period is also excluded.

15. **POLLUTION, *ASBESTOS* AND LEAD EXCLUSION**
   - **A.** *We* do not cover *bodily injury, property damage* or *personal injury* arising out of, caused by, or resulting from any of the following:
     1. The actual, alleged, or threatened discharge, dispersal, emission, escape, flowing, leakage, migration, release, or seepage of *pollutants* or other similar forms of environmental damage, regardless of where or how such may take place.
     2. The actual, alleged, or threatened exposure to *asbestos;* or the presence of *asbestos* in any place.
     3. Lead or lead contamination. This includes injury or damage caused by or through absorbing lead, chewing on, eating or otherwise ingesting lead or inhaling lead; or the contamination of, or existence of, lead in air, ground or water, or any part of a premises including, but not limited to, building materials and paint.
   - **B.** *We* do not cover any cost, expense, liability, or loss arising out of any of the following:
     1. Any demand, directive, order, or request that any *insured* or others clean up, contain, detoxify, monitor, neutralize, remove, test for, treat, or in any way assess the effects of or respond to *pollutants, asbestos,* lead or lead contamination; or
     2. Any claim or suit by, or on behalf of, any governmental authority for damages or reimbursement because of cleaning up, containing, detoxifying, monitoring, neutralizing, removing, testing for, treating, or in any way assessing the effects of or responding to *pollutants, asbestos,* lead or lead contamination.
   - **C. If this policy covers a *residential dwelling,* the following provisions apply:**
     1. *We* do not cover *bodily injury* or *property damage* arising out of any consequences of the failure of any *insured* to disclose the presence of any *lead-based paint* or *lead-based paint hazard* at the time of the sale or lease of a *residential dwelling.*
     2. *We* will not defend any action which arises out of such failure.

Glossary
Lead-based paint means paint or other surface coatings that contain lead equal to or in excess of 1.0 milligram per square centimeter or 0.5 percent by weight.

Lead-based paint hazard means any condition that causes exposure to lead from lead-contaminated dust, lead-contaminated soil, or lead-contaminated paint that is deteriorated or present in accessible surfaces, friction surfaces, or impact surfaces that would result in adverse human health effects as established by the appropriate Federal agency.

Residential dwelling means:
1. A single-family dwelling, including attached structures such as porches and stoops; or
2. A single-family dwelling unit in a structure that contains more than one separate residential dwelling unit, and in which each unit is used or occupied, or intended to be used or occupied, in whole or in part, as the residence of one or more persons.

16. **PROFESSIONAL EXCLUSION**
We do not cover *bodily injury, property damage* or *personal injury* arising out of the rendering or failing to render any sort of professional service.

17. **WORKERS COMPENSATION AND SIMILAR LAWS EXCLUSION**
We do not cover *bodily injury* to anyone eligible to receive benefits under a disability, occupational disease, workers' compensation, or similar law when benefits are required to be provided or are voluntarily made available by any *insured.*

SECTION III • LIMITS OF LIABILITY

A. *Our* maximum total liability for all damages resulting from an *occurrence* is the limit of liability shown in the Umbrella Declarations. This applies regardless of the number of:
1. Accidents or events;
2. Claims made or suits brought;

3. *Insureds;* or

4. Persons or organizations making claims or bringing suits.

B. If the *occurrence* is covered by *underlying primary insurance, our* limit of liability under this insurance applies to any damages which exceed the limits of liability of all the *underlying primary insurance* policies together with any other collectible insurance available to the *insured.*

C. If the *occurrence* is not covered by *underlying primary insurance,* but is covered by this insurance, then *our* limit of liability applies to damages which exceed the Self-Insured Retention limit shown in the Umbrella Declarations. The *insured* shall retain this amount as self insurance.

However, this condition does not apply when the following Paragraph D, applies.

D. When coverage and payment that might otherwise have been available to the *insured* under *underlying primary insurance* (with respect to any covered *occurrence)* is not available because such *underlying primary insurance:*

1. Has been terminated, reduced in coverage, or reduced in limits (other than a reduction of aggregate limits because of claim payments); or

2. Is not payable because the *underlying insurer* is bankrupt, insolvent, or is otherwise generally relieved of making payments by judicial decree, legislation or regulation; or

3. Is not payable because the *insured* failed to comply with contractual requirements of such; then

We will pay solely as though the applicable *underlying primary insurance* is fully payable.

For example: if the otherwise covered damages are $500,000 and the subject primary policy would have provided $300,000 in payment, then *we* will pay no more than $200,000 ($500,000 less $300,000).

In such cases, *we* are not obligated to provide the defense and supplementary payments described in Section I. B, although *we* retain the right to do so.

E. This insurance applies separately to each *insured.* However, the inclusion of more than one *insured* in any claim or suit does not increase *our* limit of liability.

F. Any collected recovery or salvage will be deducted from such excess liability.

SECTION IV • CONDITIONS

1. ACTION OR SUIT AGAINST *US*
No action may be brought against *us* until all conditions in this coverage form are complied with, and until the amount of the *insured's* obligation (payable under this insurance) has been determined by judgment in trial or by agreement made with *our* written consent.

No right exists here for *you* or others to make *us* party to an action against any *insured.*

2. APPEALS

A. If the *insured* or the *insured's underlying insurer* elects not to appeal a judgment which exceeds the *applicable underlying limit, we* may do so.

B. If *we* do, *we* will pay all costs of the appeal. *We* will also pay all costs on appeals related to the defense of the *insured* as provided under Defense of Claims or Suits (Section I. B). These sums are in addition to the limit of liability for this insurance. In no event shall *our* liability for *ultimate net loss* exceed the limit of liability for this insurance.

3. BANKRUPTCY
Bankruptcy of the *insured* or the *insured's* estate does not relieve *us* of *our* obligations under this insurance.

4. CANCELLATION AND TERMINATION

A. *Your* Right to Cancel.
You may cancel this policy by: surrendering the policy to *us* or *our* agent or by mailing *us* or *our* agent notice stating a subsequent cancellation date for the policy.

A minimum earned premium may apply.

If *you* secure insurance with another insurer to replace *our* insurance and do not pay the premium, or installment payment, for this insurance when due: this insurance terminates at the time such other insurance becomes effective.

B. *Our* Right to Cancel or Terminate.

1. We may cancel this insurance by mailing or delivering to *you* written notice of cancellation at least:

   a. 10 days before the effective date of cancellation if *we* cancel for nonpayment of premium; or

   b. 30 days before the effective date of cancellation if *we* cancel for any other reason.

   Notice of cancellation will state the effective date of cancellation. The policy period will end on that date.

2. *We* will make or deliver *our* notice to *you* at *your* last mailing address known to *us.* If notice is mailed, proof of mailing will be sufficient proof of notice.

3. If this insurance is cancelled, *we* will send *you* any premium refund due. All premium returns are calculated pro rata.

5. CHANGES
This coverage form contains all the agreements between *you* and *us* concerning the insurance afforded. This coverage form's terms can be amended or waived only by endorsement issued by *us* and made a part of this coverage form.

6. CONCEALMENT / MISREPRESENTATION / FRAUD
This coverage form is void if, either before or after an

occurrence or claim, any *insured* misrepresents or knowingly conceals any material fact or circumstance, commits fraud, or swears falsely relating to any aspect of this insurance (including the information *we* relied upon in issuing this contract). However, if *we* specifically choose not to declare this coverage form void, *we* do not provide insurance here to, or for the benefit of, any such *insureds.*

7. CONFORMITY WITH STATUTE

It is agreed by *us* that the provisions in this coverage form are amended to conform to all applicable statutory requirements.

8. DUTIES OF *INSUREDS* – WHAT TO DO IN CASE OF CLAIM, INJURY, *OCCURRENCE,* OR SUIT

You and any other involved *insured* must do all of the following:

A. Immediately notify *us* of all relevant circumstances relating to a claim or any incident which may result in a claim, with all necessary information. For example: who *you* are; the time, place, and circumstances of the injury or *occurrence;* the names and addresses of injured persons and witnesses.

B. Immediately send *us* copies of all bills, documents, notices, papers, or summonses related to any claim or suit brought against any *insured* which may result in a claim against this insurance.

C. Cooperate with *us* in matters relevant to the claim or suit. Assist *us* in: conducting suits, including by attending hearings and trials and giving evidence; enforcing any *insured's* rights of contribution or indemnity against others; investigating *occurrences;* making settlements; obtaining records (or other information) or the attendance of witnesses.

D. Submit to examination and provide statements under oath and sign and swear to such. If more than one person is examined, *we* reserve the right to examine and receive statements from each person separately and out of the presence of the others. *We* also reserve the right to video record any examination.

E. When *we* believe that a claim may exceed the *underlying primary insurance, we* may join with the *insured* and the *underlying insurer* in the investigation, settlement and defense of all claims and suits in connection with such *occurrence.* In such event, the *insured* must cooperate with *us.*

F. Refrain from voluntarily making payments, assuming obligations, or incurring defense, investigative, or any other expenses – unless with *our* specific written authorization to do so (otherwise such undertakings will be at the *insured's* own expense and *we* will not pay for them).

Failure to comply with these (or other conditions) can alter or void *our* obligations in this coverage form.

9. LIBERALIZATION

This coverage form is automatically extended to include provisions approved during the policy period or within 45 days prior to its inception, which would broaden coverage in this coverage form, if such are not subject to additional premium or concurrent with coverage restrictions.

10. MAINTENANCE OF UNDERLYING INSURANCE

The insurance afforded by each policy listed in the Schedule of Underlying Insurance in the Umbrella Declarations will be maintained for the full term of this insurance. This provision does not apply to the reduction of the aggregate limit or limits due to payment of claims for *bodily injury, personal injury,* or *property damage.* As these policies expire, *you* will renew them at limits at least equal to the expiring limits of insurance.

If *you* fail to comply with the requirements in the preceding paragraph, this insurance is not invalidated. However, in the event of a loss, *we* will pay only to the extent that *we* would have paid had *you* so complied in accordance with Section III D.

You must give *us* written notice of any change in the *underlying primary insurance* as respects:

A. Coverage.

B. Limits of insurance.

C. Termination of any coverage.

D. Exhaustion of aggregate limits.

11. OTHER INSURANCE

This insurance is excess over any other valid and collectible insurance whether such other insurance is stated to be primary, contributing, excess, contingent or otherwise. This provision does not apply to a policy bought specifically to apply in excess of this insurance.

12. RECOVERY FROM OTHERS

If *we* make a payment under this insurance, *insureds* will assist *us* and the *underlying insurer* in recovering what *we* paid by using the *insured's* right to recovery. Reimbursement will be made in the following order:

A. First, to any interests (including any *insured)* who has paid any amount in excess of the limits of liability of this insurance;

B. Next, to *us;* and

C. Then to any interests (including the *insured* and the *underlying insurer)* as are entitled to claim the remainder, if any.

A different order may apply if agreed upon by all interests. Expenses incurred in the process of recovery will be divided among all interests according to the ratio of their respective recoveries.

13. SEPARATION OF *INSUREDS*

Except with respect to *our* limit of liability and any rights or duties specifically assigned to *you,* this insurance applies separately to each *insured* against whom claim is made or suit is brought.

14. TIME OF INCEPTION / COVERAGE PERIOD
The time of inception and expiration is 12:01 A.M. Standard Time at the mailing address shown in the Declarations.

15. TRANSFER OF *YOUR* RIGHTS AND DUTIES UNDER THIS INSURANCE
Your rights and duties under this insurance may not be transferred without *our* written consent except in the case of *your* death.

If *you* die, *your* rights and duties will be transferred to *your* legal representative but only while acting within the scope of duties as *your* legal representative. Until *your* legal representative is appointed, anyone having proper temporary custody of *your* property will have *your* rights and duties but only with respect to that property.

SECTION V • GLOSSARY

The following words are defined for the purposes of this insurance:

Aircraft
Aircraft means any contrivance used or designed for flight, but does not include model or hobby craft unless used or designated to carry cargo or persons.

Asbestos
Asbestos means the mineral in any form, including but not limited to fibers or dust.

Applicable Underlying Limit
Applicable underlying limit means:

1. If the policies of *underlying primary insurance* apply to the *occurrence,* the greater of:
   A. The amount of insurance stated in the policies of *underlying primary insurance* in the Declarations or any other available insurance less the amount by which any aggregate limit so stated has been reduced solely due to payment of claims; or
   B. The Self Insured Retention shown in the Declarations; or
2. If the policies of *underlying primary insurance* do not apply to the *occurrence,* the amount stated in the Declarations as the Self Insured Retention.

The limits of insurance in any policy of *underlying primary insurance* will apply even if:

1. The *underlying insurer* claims the *insured* failed to comply with any condition of the policy; or
2. The *underlying insurer* becomes bankrupt or insolvent.

Bodily Injury
Bodily injury means bodily harm, sickness, or disease sustained by a person during the coverage period, including death at any time, resulting from such, caused by a covered *occurrence.*

Business
Business means any occupation, profession, trade or commercial activity, including childcare activities undertaken for a fee or other payment.

If MPL 101 is listed in the Declarations, *business* does not include farming activities.

Electronic Aggression
Electronic aggression means harassment or bullying done by way of any type of electronic means including, but not limited to: blogs, chat rooms, email, instant messaging, social networking or text messaging.

Insured
Insured means:

1. *You* and the following if residents of *your* household:
   A. *Your* spouse.
   B. *Your* or *your* spouse's relatives.
   C. Anyone under the age of 21 in *your* care or the care of a resident relative.
2. A full time student, as defined by the school, who was a resident of *your* household before moving out to attend school, provided that such student is under the age of:
   A. 24 and is *your* or *your* spouse's relative; or
   B. 21 and in *your* care or that of a resident relative.
3. Any other persons with respect to their liability because of acts of an *insured* described in the preceding Paragraphs 1 and 2.

Motor Vehicle
Motor vehicle means any self-propelled land vehicle, semi-trailer or trailer including any equipment or machinery attached to such.

Occurrence
Occurrence means an accident, including continuous or repeated exposure to substantially the same general harmful conditions, or an offense listed in the definition of *personal injury.*

Occurrence does not include actual or alleged misrepresentation or omissions of any kind in the sale of real or personal property.

Pollutants
Pollutants are any gaseous, liquid, solid, or thermal contaminant or irritant, including acids, alkalis, chemicals, fumes, smoke, soot, vapors, and waste (including materials to be reclaimed, reconditioned, or recycled).

Personal Injury
Personal injury means injury, other than *bodily injury,* arising out of one or more of the following offenses committed during the policy period:

1. False arrest, detention or imprisonment.
2. Malicious prosecution.
3. Oral or written publication of material that: slanders or libels a person or organization; disparages a person's or organization's goods, products or services.
4. Oral or written publication of material that violates a person's right of privacy.

5. Wrongful entry into, or eviction of a person from, or invasion of the right of private occupancy of, a dwelling, room, or other private premises that the person occupies.

Property Damage
Property damage means the following which occurs during the policy period:

1. Direct physical injury to tangible property, including loss of use of such property (the loss of use is deemed to occur at the time of such direct physical injury).

2. Loss of use of tangible property that is not physically injured: all such loss of use is deemed to occur at the time of the *occurrence* causing the loss.

Ultimate Net Loss
Ultimate net loss means the sum actually paid or payable due to a claim for which the *insured* is liable either by a settlement to which *we* agreed or a final judgment. Such sum will include proper adjustments for recoveries and salvage.

Underlying Primary Insurance
Underlying primary insurance means the policies listed in the Schedule of Underlying Insurance and includes:

1. Any renewal or replacement of such policies; and

2. Any other insurance available to the *insured.*

Underlying Insurer
Underlying insurer means any insurer which provides a policy listed in the Schedule of Underlying Insurance or any other insurance available to the *insured.*

You, Your and Yourself
You, your and *yourself* refer to the *insured* named in the Declarations.

We, Us and Our
We, us and *our* refer to the Insurance Company named in the Declarations.

Index